Hourglass

RICKY CLEMONS

PUBLISHED BY FIEDLI PUBLISHING, INC.

ISBN: 978-1-955622-68-4

Published by

Fideli Publishing, Inc.
119 W. Morgan St.
Martinsville, IN 46151
www.FideliPublishing.com

Table of Contents

Hourglass

Do we only have an hourglass of faith in the Lord when things don't go our way?

Do we only have an hourglass of faith to run out when the Lord doesn't answer our prayers on our time?

Do we only have an hourglass of sand to run out when it seems like our ministry is worthless?

Do we only have an hourglass of faith in the Lord if we don't get much support from our brothers and sisters in the Lord?

Do we only have an hourglass of faith in the Lord if only a few people are blessed by our ministry work in the Lord?

Do we only have an hourglass of sand to run out when we have been falsely accused, especially by our brothers or sisters in the Lord?

An hourglass of faith in the Lord is a faith that runs out when the storms come into our lives.

An hourglass of faith in the Lord is a faith that runs out when we let material things distract us from the Lord.

We don't know how much faith we have in the Lord until we are up against a wall that we cannot knock down.

The Lord truly knows if we only have an hourglass of faith in Him.

We can easily believe that our faith in the Lord can't run out like the sand in an hourglass.

Many of us Christians today are not really going through some real hard times like many of the Christians back in the Bible days.

Noah's faith in the Lord never ran out like the sand in an hourglass.

Daniel and the three Hebrew boys' faith never ran out like the sand in an hourglass.

Rahab and Esther's faith in the Lord never ran out like the sand in an hourglass.

John the Baptist's faith never ran out like the sand in an hourglass.

The Apostle Paul's faith never ran out like the sand in an hourglass.

There were many others who had faith in the Lord that didn't run out like the sand in an hourglass.

We don't want to have an hourglass of faith in the Lord who can do anything but fail us.

An hourglass of faith in the Lord has caused many people to turn their backs on the Lord.

Life in this world is like the sand running out of an hourglass.

The best life that anyone can live is to live unto the Lord Jesus Christ, even though it won't always be easy but it will surely be very rewarding to us who are saved in Jesus and receive eternal life when Jesus comes back again.

Do we only have an hourglass of faith in the Lord when disappointment seems to get the best of us?

Does our faith run out like the sand in an hourglass when we can't see our way out of a bad situation?

If our faith in the Lord runs out like the sand in an hourglass for a day, the Lord is merciful to turn the hourglass back over to the beginning for you and me to start a new day and believe that Jesus will work things out for us.

An hourglass of faith in the Lord is not the end to him, who knows how to bring our faith back to Him.

Jesus knows all of our hearts, even when our outward appearances may look like our faith isn't in the Lord and has run out like the sand in an hourglass, especially to our brothers and sisters in the church.

If you and I only have an hourglass of faith in the Lord, then our ministry would have run out by now.

Our spiritual Gifts from the Lord would have run out by now.

Our relationship with the Lord would have run out by now.

Our works for the Lord would have run out by now.

Our obedience unto the Lord would have run out by now.

An hourglass of faith in the Lord is a faith that will surely fail when the going gets tough.

An hourglass of faith in the Lord will not please the Lord to answer our prayers, because if we don't believe in Jesus how can He give us what we ask for in his name?

Do we only have an hourglass of faith in the Lord when trouble comes our way?

Does our faith in the Lord run out like the sand in an hourglass when it seems like things won't get any better in our lives?

Do we only have an hourglass of faith in the Lord when we are sick and it seems like we can't get well?

Do we only have an hourglass of faith in the Lord when life hits us with heavy blows of grief?

Does our faith in the Lord run out like the sand in an hourglass when things don't go right for us?

Do we only have an hourglass of faith in the Lord when it seems like our lives are falling apart?

An hourglass of faith in the Lord will surely run out like the sand in an hourglass.

Only the Lord can turn an hourglass of faith back over so the sand can start falling again and fall into the Lord's hands.

The Lord's almighty hands can hold the sand of another chance to give to you and me if our faith in Him has been like an hourglass that the sand has run out of.

Does our faith in the Lord run out like the sand in an hourglass when we are up against a wall of problems that never seem to end?

Does our faith in the Lord run out like the sand in an hourglass when our enemies chew us up and spit us out with hatred?

Do we only have an hourglass of faith in the Lord when frustration and stress just don't seem to leave us alone?

An hourglass of faith in the Lord will sooner or later run out.

An hourglass of faith in the Lord is no good faith to please the Lord.

You and I surely don't want to only have an hourglass of faith in the Lord.

An hourglass of faith in the Lord will surely cause us to lose our spiritual eyesight to run out like the sand in an hourglass.

We can always be thankful unto the Lord Jesus Christ who can turn the hourglass of faith back over again.

Jesus can allow the sands of His mercy and grace to fall on our lives and give us more time to live on His hourglass that could be many more years for you and me to have a mountain of faith in Him.

Does our faith in the Lord run out like the sand in an hourglass when death surrounds us with its very frightening and anxious presence to take us to the grave?

We can choose to have much faith, or an hourglass of faith, in the Lord, especially if our lives are in danger that is hard to adapt to.

Lift Up Jesus' Name in Poetry

I love to lift up Jesus' name in poetry.

Jesus has given me the gift to write poetry to uplift His holy name.

Poetry about Jesus Christ is connecting the real world to the spiritual world.

Jesus was a real man without sin when he lived in the real world.

Jesus connected the real world to the spiritual world of God.

No prophet or priest can connect the real world to the spiritual world better than Jesus Christ.

Jesus connected to the spiritual world to feed the hungry in the real world.

Jesus connected to the spiritual world to cast out demons in the real world.

Jesus connected to the spiritual world to open the eyes of the blind in the real world.

Jesus connected to the spiritual world to walk on water in the real world.

Jesus connected to the spiritual world to calm the storm in the real world.

Jesus connected to the spiritual world to heal the sick in the real world.

Jesus connected to God in the spiritual world to minister to sinners in the real world.

Jesus connected to God in the spiritual world to give Him the strength to endure His physical pain on the cross in the real world.

Jesus left the spiritual world in heaven to live in the real world on Earth.

Jesus died on the cross in the real world and He rose from the grave to go back to God in the spiritual world.

Jesus died for our sins in the real world and got the victory over our sins in the spiritual world of God.

Jesus felt all of our pain in the real world and gave it to His heavenly Father God in the spiritual world.

Jesus loves us all and wants to save us all in the real world so that He can one day come back to take us to His spiritual World in heaven if we are saved in Him.

I love to be real in my poetry that the holy spirit makes spiritual for me so I can be lifted up in the spiritual world of God and lift you up in the spiritual world of God when you read it.

God created the real world that is seen and God created the spirit world that is unseen.

God created you and me to be real people in the real world, and God will give you and me a real body for us to live forever and ever with Him in His spiritual world in heaven when Jesus Christ comes back again to receive all who love Him so real and obey Him so real in the real world.

I love to lift up Jesus' name in poetry that will take you and me up to great spiritual heights that we will never regret.

We can regret some things that we say and do in the real world, but we will never regret giving our lives to Jesus Christ.

Lift up Jesus' holy name in poetry because that will never disconnect you and me from using our life experiences to communicate to the spiritual world of God.

Jesus Is

Jesus is the King of kings.

Jesus is the Judge of judges.

Jesus is the Prince of princes.

Jesus is the Lawyer of lawyers.

Jesus is the Warrior of Warriors.

Jesus is the Builder of builders.

Jesus is the Bridge and bridges.

Jesus is the Holy Law of laws.

Jesus is the Reverent of reverence.

Jesus is the Brother of brothers.

Jesus is the Pilot of pilots.

Jesus is the Mountain of mountains.

Jesus is the Answer of answers.

Jesus is the Light of lights.

Jesus is the Way of ways.

Jesus is the Path of paths.

Jesus is the Walk of walks.

Jesus is the Order of orders.

Jesus is the Living Truth of truth.

Jesus is the Eternal Life of life.

Jesus is the Doctor of doctors.

Jesus is the Surgeon of Surgeons.

Jesus is the High Priest of the priests.

Jesus is the Healer of healers.

Jesus is the Living Waters of waters.

Jesus is the Ancient of Days of days.

Jesus is the Shepherd of shepherds.

Jesus is the Victory of victories.

Jesus is the Master of masters.

Jesus is the General of generals.

Jesus is the Captain of captains.

Jesus is the Lord of lords.

Jesus is the Author of authors.

Jesus is the Lover of lovers.

Jesus is the Teacher of teachers.

Jesus is the Authority of authorities.

Jesus is the Ruler of rulers.

Jesus is the Living Word of words.

Jesus is the Reality of realities.

Jesus is the Perfection of perfectionists.

Jesus is the Holiness of holy.

Jesus is the Righteousness of righteous.

Jesus is the Mediator of mediators.

Jesus's the Interpreter of interpreters.

Jesus is the Discerner of discerners.

Jesus is the Wisdom of the wise.

Jesus is the Knowledge of the knowledgeable.

Jesus is the Heaven of the heavens.

Jesus is the Treasure of treasures.

Jesus is the Faithful of faithfulness.

Jesus is the Star of the stars.

Jesus is the Mystery of mysteries.

Jesus is the Lamb of lambs.

Jesus is the Humility of the humble.

Jesus is the Greatest of the great.

Jesus is the Strength of the strong.

Jesus is the Glory of the glorious.

Jesus is the Grace of the graceful.

Jesus is the Credit of the creditors.

Jesus is the Riches of the rich.

Jesus is the Beauty of the beautiful.

Jesus is the Existence of all existence.

Jesus is the Helper of helpers.

Jesus is the Communicator of communicators.

Jesus is the Protector of the protectors.

Jesus is the Security of securities.

Jesus is the Foundation of foundations.

Jesus is the Counselor of counselors.

Jesus is the Social Worker of social workers.

Jesus is the Free of freedoms.

Jesus is the Caretaker of caretakers.

Jesus is the Founder of founders.

Jesus is the Servant of the servants.

Jesus is the Listener of the listeners.

Jesus is the Home of homes.

Jesus is the Joy of joys.

Jesus is the Comfort of comforters.

Jesus is the Revealer of revealers.

Jesus is the Living door of doors.

Jesus is the Possible of possibilities.

Jesus is the Employer of employers.

Jesus is the Parent of parents.

Jesus's the Conductor of conductors.

Jesus is the Groom of grooms.

Jesus is the Giver of givers.

Jesus is the Friend of friends.

Jesus is the Forgiver of forgivers.

Jesus is the Nurse of nurses.

Jesus is the Psychiatrist of psychiatrists.

Jesus is the Psychologist of psychologists.

Jesus is the Scientist of scientists.

Jesus is the Provider of providers.

Jesus is the Gardener of gardeners.

Jesus is the Farmer of farmers.

Jesus is the Astronaut of astronauts.

Jesus is the Living Song of songs.

Jesus is the Living Prize of prizes.

Jesus is the Living True Story of stories.

Jesus is the Supreme of supremes.

Jesus Christ is Real

Jesus is real, just like you and I know that we are real to see, taste, hear touch and smell.

Jesus was a real, sinless man from head to toe when he lived here on Earth.

Many people don't believe that Jesus is real and that he is our Lord and savior.

Jesus was real, and He gave up His life on the cross for our sins.

You and I can see that we are real and not make believe, and Jesus is forevermore real than you and I can ever be.

It will be real when Jesus Christ comes back again on the Clouds Of Glory with all of his heavenly angels, who are also real.

It will be real when Jesus raises the righteous dead to receive eternal life.

You and I are real and will not believe that we are not real to live, eat, drink and move about here and there.

We can surely believe that Jesus Christ is the proof that God is real, because Jesus is the son of God, who the devil could not defeat when Jesus lived here on Earth.

We can look at ourselves and see that we are real.

We have a real body to live in every day.

We can believe that Jesus Christ was a real man in this world where we see and live with real people.

If Jesus Christ is not real, then we are not real either and everything we see is imaginary.

Only a fool would believe that Jesus Christ is not real to make themselves a companion to the devil, who is real and loves to try to deceive you and me into thinking that Jesus is not real.

Jesus was real when the angels didn't exist.

Jesus existed before the devil and his fallen angels, who know that they are real to tempt you and me to do evil every day.

We believe that life is real because we love to live.

Life is from the Lord, who doesn't make anyone ill in the mind and body, Jesus made the mind and the body real to be a unity.

Jesus Christ is real and He made you and me real people who He loves.

Only Jesus Can Do That

Jesus says, "If you love me you will keep my Commandments," but Commandments can't save us from our sins.

The Commandments can't work things out for us, only Jesus Christ can do that.

The Commandments can't protect us from harm and danger, only Jesus can do that.

It's always good to keep the Commandments that Jesus Christ kept when He lived here on Earth without sin in His flesh.

The Commandments can't cleanse us of our sins, only Jesus can do that.

The Commandments can't redeem us, only Jesus can do that.

The Commandments point our sins out to us, but Jesus gives us the strength to not sin against Him.

The Commandments can't forgive us of our sins, only Jesus can do that.

The Commandments can't cast our sins into the deepest sea, only Jesus can do that.

The Commandments can't give us a second chance, only Jesus can do that.

The Commandments can't raise anyone from the dead, only Jesus Christ will do that when He comes back again to raise His righteous dead from the grave.

The Commandments can't change the righteous living from mortal to immortal, only Jesus will do that when He comes back again.
The Commandments can't give us the strength to go through our trials, only Jesus can bring us through.

The Commandments can't heal us, only Jesus can do that.

The Commandments didn't die on the cross for our sins.

When Jesus died on the cross for our sins, the Commandments didn't raise Him from the grave — the Holy Spirit raised Jesus from the grave.

The Commandments can't take us to Heaven one day soon, only Jesus Christ will do that if we are saved in Him.

If the Commandments could save us from our sins, then Jesus Christ would have had no need to give up His life on the cross for our sins.

We must pray to Jesus and not pray to the Commandments — they can't answer our prayers.

We can't put the Commandments above Jesus Christ who is the truth and grace of God.

The Bible says that we must believe in Jesus Christ to be saved.

The Bible did not say that we must believe in the Commandments to be saved.

The Commandments are always good to keep, but they can't make us right with God.

Only the righteousness of Jesus Christ can make us right with God.

Under the Sky

Under the sky is where love is not so sure to grow up and mature.

Under the sky, life experiences can be like riding on a roller coaster.

Under the sky, time is not so sure to be on our side when we need it.

Under the sky is where we can't be so sure about anything in this world.

Under the sky, the great and small have problems that are not always solved.

Under the sky, life is not so sure to give us another day to live.

Under the sky is where change can be painful.

Under the sky is where logic can be degraded.

Under the sky is where hope can be helpless.

Under the sky is where friends can turn their backs on you and me.

Under the sky is where we can't be so sure about ourselves.

Under the sky is where ignorance can be praised.

Under the sky is where knowledge can be combative.

Under the sky is where wisdom can be foolish to a fool.

Under the sky is where Jesus Christ once lived to show to the world God's love.

Under the sky is where Jesus Christ once lived to save us from our sins.

Under the sky is where sin can look like an angel from heaven.

Under the sky is where the wicked have made their homes.

Under the sky is where the natural can be like an uncommon thing to the unnatural.

Under the sky is where a marriage can seem like it's for sale at a cheap price.

Under the sky is where doing something bad is like a good thing to do.

Under the sky is where religion can be like a hustler who gambles with people's souls that Jesus loves to save.

Under the sky is where Jesus Christ once lived among sinners like you and me to show the world that there is a true Living God who wants to have a relationship with the human race.

Under the sky is where death can be like a king sitting on his throne where everyone can see him joking and laughing at life.

Under the sky is where we were born to one day die, which is like throwing water on a campfire to make it burn out on a cold night.

Under the sky is where Jesus Christ once lived without sin as He took on our trespasses and inequities and was like a lamb in a den of hungry wolves.

Under the sky a good day is for us, and a bad day is against us, which is like a split personality that changes on us.

Under the sky is where Jesus Christ once lived and never changed on anyone because Jesus is the same yesterday, today and tomorrow.

Jesus is like a good day every day, and only Jesus can make the day be a blessing for us in some kind of way.

Under the sky is where feelings can get trampled down like a crushed egg.

Under the sky is where beauty can fade away like it never existed before old age.

Under the sky is where a war can look so meaningless when it's all over, like it was never fought.

Under the sky is where an actor can be a good pretender and captivate an audience to make someone believe the pretense is real.

Under the sky is where Jesus Christ once lived with no pretense and was real like the deep waters under a bridge that make the bridge very useful to cross over.

Under the sky is where accomplishments can break into pieces, like when a good name is ruined.

Under the sky is where wealth can be a burden to a rich person, like being lost in a forest.

Under the sky is where faith in the Lord Jesus Christ can be out of date for unbelievers who believe and live by their eyesight day after day.

Under the sky is where history can be like wallowing in mud that only clean water can wash off of our bodies.

Under the sky is like trying to clean up the past, and dress it up for the present.

Under the sky is where violence and killings can be like a lifestyle that is accepted into society.

Under the sky is where dreams can be questioned and might not give you the right answer.

Under the sky is where Jesus Christ once lived and was like a good dream passing through every generation.

Under the sky is where education can be the right answer to every problem, to be like a vault in a bank that is under tight security.

A professional criminal may very well break into that vault, which shows that education can also be used for evil practices.

Under the sky is where Jesus Christ once lived to minister to and educate His disciples with the word of God, who is good all the time with the right answer to every problem.

Jesus educated His disciples to do good deeds, but Judas chose to do an evil deed by betraying Jesus Christ.

Judas used his education for evil.

Jesus educated Judas with his ministry and then Judas used that against Him for evil.

Under the sky is where limits exist because we were born in sin.

This is like if we see a poisonous snake in our pathway it would be best to wait until the snake crawls far away out of our eyesight before we walk down the pathway.

The poisonous snake is our limit for us to not go near to it in our pathway.

Under the sky is where we have limits to add more years to our lives.

It's the Lord's Mercy

The Lord shows mercy on whoever He wants to show mercy on.

When a hurricane passes by us, it's the Lord's mercy upon us.

When a tornado doesn't touch down on us, it's the Lord's mercy upon us.

When we are spared from a bad accident, it's the Lord's mercy upon us.

When a stray bullet passes by a little child, it's the Lord's mercy upon that child.

When we get well from a sickness, it's the Lord's mercy upon us.

When we wake up in the morning, it's the Lord's mercy upon us.

The Lord shows His mercy, even upon animals.

When a sick horse gets well, it's the Lord's mercy upon the horse.

When a sick dog gets well, it's the Lord's mercy upon the dog.

When we accomplish things in our lives, it's the Lord's mercy upon us.

It's the Lord's mercy that gives us another chance to make it right with Him.

It's the Lord's mercy that gives us another chance to make things right with our neighbors.

It's the Lord's mercy that gives us another chance to make things right in our marriages.

It's the Lord's mercy that gives us another chance to make things right in our families.

When a doctor tells you that your cancer is gone, it's the Lord's mercy upon you.

When your life is spared from getting killed, it's the Lord's mercy upon you.

When you come back home from the war, it's the Lord's mercy upon you.

It's the Lord's mercy that gives us a chance to wise up and live right.

If we live to get old, it's the Lord's mercy upon us.

The Lord shows His mercy on whoever He wants to show His mercy on.

We can't question the Lord about why He allows many good young people's lives to be cut short.

God's mercy can be like a mystery that we can't solve.

We can always thank the Lord for his mercy that we don't deserve from Him.

We can always thank the Lord for His mercy that means we can rise above and go beyond our trials.

We can't question the Lord about who He wants to give His mercy to.

We may never understand why the Lord allows good people to suffer for a long time from an illness.

We can be thankful unto the Lord for His mercy that a wish and crossing your fingers and Magic can't measure up to — these things are powerless compared to God's mercy.

Luck, a wish, crossing your fingers and magic will sooner or later run out of zeal compared to the Lord's mercy that energizes time to give us more time to live our lives unto the Lord before it's too late.

Can't Get Rid Of

Technology can't get rid of evil desires.

Science can't get rid of evil desires.

Education can't get rid of evil desires.

Religious ceremonies can't get rid of evil desires.

Astrology can't get rid of evil desires.

Horoscopes can't get rid of evil desires.

The church can't get rid of evil desires.

Good health can't get rid of evil desires.

Nature can't get rid of evil desires.

Common sense can't get rid of evil desires.

Money can't get rid of evil desires.

Talents can't get rid of evil desires.

Skills can't get rid of evil desires.

Intelligence can't get rid of evil desires.

Beauty can't get rid of evil desires.

Only Jesus Christ can get rid of evil desires.

If we are born again in Jesus Christ, he will cleanse us of our evil desires and we won't have any more evil desires to willfully sin against the Lord.

If we are saved in Jesus Christ, we won't want to have an evil desire to sin against Jesus, our Lord.

Only Jesus has the power to help us to overcome evil desires.

Accomplishments can't get rid of evil desires.

Success can't get rid of evil desires.

Prosperity can't get rid of evil desires.

Freedom can't get rid of evil desires.

Only Jesus Christ can get rid of evil desires that try to control our lives, but this cannot happen if we don't confess and repent of our sins unto to Jesus Christ and live a renewed life in the spirit of God.

The Lord Won't Allow

The Lord won't allow the devil to tempt us with more than what we can handle.

The Lord knows if we can't handle a lot of stress.

The Lord knows if we can't handle a lot of pressure.

The Lord knows if we can't handle a lot of fear.

The Lord knows if we can't handle a lot of drama.

The Lord knows if we can't handle a lot of excitement.

The Lord knows if we can't handle a lot of grief.

The Lord knows if we can't handle a lot of Gossip.

The Lord knows if we can't handle a lot of rejection.

The Lord knows if we can't handle a lot of lies.

The Lord knows if we can't handle a lot of deception.

The Lord knows if we can't handle a lot of neglect.

The Lord knows if we can't handle a lot of abuse.

The Lord knows if we can't handle a lot of Violence.

The Lord knows if we can't handle a lot of sickness.

The Lord knows if we can't handle a lot of Heartache.

The Lord knows if we can't handle a lot of pain.

The Lord knows if we can't handle a lot of bias.

The Lord knows if we can't handle a lot of exposure.

The Lord won't allow the devil to tempt us with more than what we can bear.

The Lord knows if we can't bear a lot of bad news.

The Lord knows if we can't bear a lot of frustration.

The Lord knows if we can't bear a lot of joking.

The Lord knows if we can't bear a lot of pretense.

The Lord knows if we can't bear a lot of nagging.

The Lord knows if we can't bear a lot of killing.

The Lord knows if we can't bear a lot of talking.

The Lord knows if we can't bear a lot of publicity.

The Lord knows if we can't bear a lot of height.

The Lord knows if we can't bear a lot of abandonment.

The Lord knows if we can't bear a lot of manipulation.

The Lord knows if we can't bear a lot of isolation.

The Lord knows that if we can't bear a lot of anxiety.

The Lord knows if we can't bear a lot of favoritism.

The Lord knows if we can't bear a lot of fame.

The Lord knows if we can't bear a lot of mistakes.

The Lord knows if we can't bear a lot of misfortune.

The Lord knows if we can't bear a lot of disappointments.

The devil would love to overtake us with his temptations and destroy us, but the Lord loves us so much that He will not allow the devil to tempt us with more than what we can bear.

The Lord knows how much we can bear.

We don't know how much we can bear.

We can choose to wreck our own lives and the Lord can allow us to bear it and live with it until we die.

You and I can't be too lost in sin for Jesus to not find us and bring us back to Him, who bore all of our sins on the cross so that you and I can bear what He allows us to bear.

Jesus Christ won't allow evil things to be too much for us to bear, and that makes the devil have a lost cause against us with his temptations.

The Lord won't allow any of His children to be tempted with more than what we can bear, even if we are facing death.

That is hard to do, but not hard for the Lord to pass death by us.

There is Only One Me

There is only one me who can take care of me or not take care of me.

There is only one me who can accept me for who I am or not accept me for who I am.

There is only one me who can be true to me or not be true to me.

There is only one me who can look out for me or not look out for me.

There is only one me who can do me good or not do me good.

There is only one me who can lift me up or tear me down.

There is only one me who can feel good about me or feel bad about me.

There is only one me who can trust me or not trust me.

There is only one me who can be happy for me or not be happy for me.

There is only one me who can love me or hate me.

There is only one me who can love God more than me or love me more than God.

There is only one me who can live my life to please me or live my life to please God.

There is only one me who can speak words of life or speak words of death.

There is only one me who can believe in Jesus Christ or not believe in Jesus Christ.

There is only one me who can pick up my cross and follow Jesus Christ or not pick up my cross and not follow Jesus Christ.

There is only one me who can deny Jesus Christ or not deny Jesus Christ.

There is only one me who can confess and repent of my sins unto Jesus Christ or not confess and not repent of my sins unto Jesus Christ.

There is only one me who can steer my final destiny to heaven or hell.

There is only one me who can listen to and obey the voice of God's holy spirit or not listen to and not obey the voice of God's holy spirit.

There is only one me who God will judge and hold accountable for my choices.

There is only one me and no one else can be me and take my place to surrender or not surrender my life to Jesus Christ.

There is only one me who has a shadow that moves when I move to prove that my shadow is always true to me and lets me know that I need to always be true to Jesus Christ.

There is only one me, even though there are many other people who have my same name.

Jesus wants to save me as if I was the only sinner who needs to be saved.

There is only one me who can be real with you or pretend with you.

There is only one me who can love you or hate you.

There is only one me who can dream or not dream.

There is only one me in this world.

There is only one me in the land of the living.

There is only one me who can do good or do evil.

There is only one me who God created.

There is only one me whose time can run out.

There is only one me who can be a good influence or a bad influence on you.

There is only one me who can chase the wind and catch nothing.

There is only one me and this world doesn't revolve around me.

There is only one me who will answer to God.

There is only one me who God loves, even if I don't love me.

There is only one me who God knew before I was born.

There is only one me who God predestined to be here today.

There is only one me who has a free will to love God or not love God.

There is only one me who God created in His image.

There is only one me who can make this world a better place to live in.

There is only one me who is not better than you.

There is only one me who God doesn't love more than you.

This World is So Unpredictable

This world is so unpredictable.

We just don't know what will happen next.

We don't know when there will be another earthquake.

We don't know when there will be another government shutdown.

We don't know when there will be another cyber attack.

We don't know when there will be another hurricane.

We don't know when there will be another tornado.

We don't know when there will be another wildfire.

We don't know when there will be another flood.

We don't know when there will be another mass shooting.

We don't know when there will be another drive-by shooting.

We don't know when there will be another baby being born.

We don't know when there will be another murder.

We don't know when there will be another cult.

We don't know when there will be another accident.

We don't know when there will be another ice storm.

We don't know when there will be another snow blizzard.

We don't know when there will be another sinkhole.

We don't know when there will be another mudslide.

We don't know when there will be another war.

We don't know when there will be another person giving their life to the Lord.

We don't know when there will be another person turning in his or her back on the Lord.

We don't know when there will be another virus.

We don't know when there will be another drought.

We don't know when there will be another Nobel Prize winner.

We don't know when there will be another millionaire.

We don't know when there will be another discovery.
We don't know when there will be another mystery.

We don't know when there will be another billionaire.

We don't know when there will be another great legend.

We don't know when there will be another theft.

We don't know when there will be another fraud.

We don't know when there will be another invention.

We don't know when there will be another volcano eruption.

We don't know when there will be another best-selling author.

This world is so unpredictable.

We just don't know what a new day will bring to us.

Mr. Selfishness and Mr. Repent

One day, Mr. Selfishness and Mr. Repent met up with each other on the borderline of Heaven and Hell.

They both had been waiting for this moment to face each other so they could clear up their differences.

When they met up with each other, Mr. Selfishness said to Mr. Repent, "I am not going to repent unto Jesus, because I am perfect in my own eyes. I see that I can do nothing wrong."

Mr. Repent responded to Mr. Selfishness saying, "Your selfish attitude toward Jesus means there is no place in heaven for you to spread your self-centered words."

Mr. Repent continued, saying to Mr. Selfishness, "Repenting is the only way for you to come to Jesus. Give your heart to Him before it's too late for you."

Mr. Selfishness refused to believe what Mr. Repent said to him, so he crossed over the border into hell.

When Mr. Selfishness entered hell, he realized that Mr. Repent had been so right about everything and that you must repent unto Jesus Christ to cross over the border into heaven.

He realized that only those who have repented of their sins are saved in Jesus Christ, who created heaven and hell.

Jesus created heaven, where Mr. Repent will go to one day, and Jesus created hell, where Mr. Selfishness will stay because he refused to repent of his sins unto Jesus Christ.

A New Day and a New Start

A new day and a new start to love the Lord.

A new day and a new start to obey the Lord.

 A new day and a new start to pray to the Lord.

A new day and a new start to read the Bible.

A new day and a new start to believe in the Lord.

A new day and a new start to trust the Lord.

A new day and a new start to depend on the Lord.

A new day and a new start to have hope in the Lord.

A new day and a new start to be a witness of the Lord.

A new day and a new start to live unto the Lord.

A new day and a new start to talk about the Lord.

A new day and a new start to give all the glory and praise to the Lord.

A new day and a new start to have a relationship with the Lord.

A new day and a new start to choose the Lord.

A new day and a new start to have faith in the Lord.

A new day and a new start to give our hearts to the Lord.

A new day and a new start to keep our minds on the Lord.

A new day and a new start to give our problems to the Lord.

A new day and a new start to give our all to the Lord.

A new day and a new start to listen to the Lord.

A new day and a new start to work for the Lord.

A new day and a new start to uplift the Lord.

A new day and a new start to not deny the Lord Jesus Christ.

No One Can

No one can strengthen me more than you, O Lord.

No one can be patient with me more than you, O Lord.

No one can bless my life more than you, O Lord.

No one can change my life better than you, O Lord.

No one can love me more than you, O Lord.

No one can help me more than you, O Lord.

No one can motivate me better than you, O Lord.

No one can encourage me better than you, O Lord.

No one can support me better than you, O Lord.

No one can understand me better than you, O Lord.

No one can talk to me more than you, O Lord.

No one can listen to me more than you, O Lord.

No one can know me better than you, O Lord.

No one can be for me more than you, O Lord.

No one can be honest with me more than you, O Lord.

No one can be a friend to me better than you, O Lord.

No one can be real with me better than you, O Lord.

No one can lift me up more than you, O Lord.

No one can be happy for me more than you, O Lord.

No one can cheer me up more than you, O Lord.

No one can touch my heart more than you, O Lord.

We Are All Vulnerable To

We are all vulnerable to the unknown.

We are all vulnerable to the uncertain.

We are all vulnerable to the unpredictable.

We are all vulnerable to dissatisfaction.

We are all vulnerable to criticism.

We are all vulnerable to failure.

We are all vulnerable to grief.

We are all vulnerable to fear.

We are all vulnerable to flaws.

We are all vulnerable to mistakes.

We are all vulnerable to habits.

We are all vulnerable to selfishness.

We are all vulnerable to grudges.

We are all vulnerable to pain.

We are all vulnerable to sickness.

We are all vulnerable to death.

We are all vulnerable to ignorance.

We are all vulnerable to opinions.

We are all vulnerable to trouble.

We are all vulnerable to prejudice.

We are all vulnerable to misfortunes.

We are all vulnerable to mischief.

We are all vulnerable to hate.

We are all vulnerable to lies.

We are all vulnerable to pretense.

We are all vulnerable to rejection.

We are all vulnerable to harm.

We are all vulnerable to danger.

We are all vulnerable to natural disasters.

We are all vulnerable to disappointments.

We are all vulnerable to giving up.

We are all vulnerable to sinning against God.

It's Always Good to Help Someone

It's always good to help someone if you are able to help someone, because when you help someone else you help yourself to not be selfish.

Helping someone else also helps you and me get our minds off of ourselves.

Helping someone else is helping that person to not be selfish.

When Jesus Christ lived here on earth, He helped so many people take the first step to believing in Him and being saved so they would not get left behind and lost in their sins.

It's always good to help someone if you are able to help someone get through his or her misfortune and not judge that person if he or she is not stable.

When you and I help someone else who needs our help, we find favor with the Lord who gives us the power to help someone else as well as ourselves so that we can get beyond the bitter and sour times in our lives.

Meeting People Where They Are

Meeting people where they are is a challenge to you and me, who are not all-knowing to succeed in meeting everyone where they are.

Meeting people where they are is not always easy to do, because people are different and can take you and me the wrong way.

We need the Lord to help us to meet people where they are in their lives that can be complicated without Jesus being in their lives.

When Jesus Christ lived on earth, He met people where they were in their lives and ministered to them.

Meeting people where they are is a humbling experience for you and me to not beleive that we are too high up to come down on an uneducated person's level and meet him or her where they are.

Meeting people where they are is what Jesus did.

When we pray to Jesus, who is in the highest heights of heaven, He hears our prayers and meet us where we are.

No one can meet people where they are better than Jesus Christ.

Proof of

Many people will say something when they don't have any proof of what they say.

Having proof of something can back up what we say.

Doing what we say is proving what we say.

It can make us feel so good when we can prove what we say to others.

Proof is a sure thing to cause you and me to believe the truth.

Proof is a sure thing to convince anyone to do the right thing.

You can give some people proof of what you say, but they still won't believe you.

Proof can be challenged every day by people who won't accept the facts.

Many people won't believe you and me if we don't have any proof of what we say.

The Bible is proof of who God is.

The Bible is proof of what God says to us.

The Bible is proof of the way that we should live our lives.

The Bible is proof of what is right and what is wrong.

The Bible is proof of what is good and what is evil.

The Bible is proof of Jesus Christ being the Son of God.

The Bible is proof of Jesus Christ being the light of the world.

The Bible is proof that Jesus Christ gave up His life on the cross to save us from our sins.

The Bible is proof that Jesus Christ rose from the grave with a victory over the grave and death.

The Bible is proof of the prophets of God, as well as the false prophets.

The Bible is proof of the devil and his demons.

The Bible is proof that Jesus Christ will come back again.

The Bible is proof of the truth about everything in this world.

If you and I are speaking words according to the Holy Bible, it proves that we are speaking the truth.

If you and I are living our lives unto Jesus Christ, it proves that we are born again in the spirit of God, to worship Him in spirit and truth.

A lawyer needs proof to win his or her case in court.

The church is proof that Jesus Christ will come back again and take His church church folks to heaven for being saved in Him.

This is the proof of salvation for all men, women, boys and girls.

I Am Rich

I am rich with the Lord giving me life, health and strength — that is great wealth.

I am rich with the Lord giving me all that I need — that is great wealth, surely indeed.

I am rich with being satisfied in my life — that is great wealth from my Lord Jesus Christ.

I am rich with my faith and trust in the Lord — that is great wealth which will one day mean I get my reward in heaven.

I am rich in being saved in the Lord — that is great wealth for me to know that I am not spiritually poor.

I am rich with victory that the Lord has given me through His victory over death and the grave.

Jesus overcame death to set me free from eternal death, because He came to this world to save my soul, and that is great wealth for the Holy Angels to behold.

I am rich with a free will that the Lord has given me to choose — this is surely great wealth to last all of my life that I choose to love and obey the Lord.

Writing is Not Always Easy

Writing is not always easy, even for many people who have the gift to write.

Many gifted writers will sometimes not be able to think of good words to write.

Many gifted writers will sometimes forget some words to write.

Many gifted writers will not always be able to think about all of their life experiences and then write about them.

Many gifted writers will sometimes write words that people will doubt.

Every writer wants their words to get attention.

Every writer wants their words to be accepted.

Every writer wants their words to touch people's hearts.

Every writer wants people to read what they have written in their books.

Whether writing fiction or nonfiction, every writer will sometimes feel some stress from writing.

Whether writing fiction or nonfiction, every writer will sometimes feel like their words are not complete.

Whether writing fiction or nonfiction, every writer will sometimes not be satisfied with the words that they write.

Writing is not always easy for even gifted writers.

Many gifted writers have written best-selling books, but they still may feel like they should have added some words or left out some words out of their books.

Writing can be a humbling experience that lets every writer know that they don't know it all.

Writing can be very challenging sometimes, especially when writers need more facts to prove what they write is true.

Writing has no age limit — even a child may have the gift to write and move hearts to change.

Every writer has his or her own special way of writing words, whether they're an experienced writer or an inexperienced writer.

Even the most gifted writers may have some inexperience and not be able to deeply touch someone's heart and make them want to change their lives for the better.

Many people read the Bible that was written by holy men of God.

All of the words God gave to them are true, even though many people don't believe that the Bible is true.

Those Bible writers were inspired by God to write words that tell us the truth about God.

Those Bible writers were inspired by God to write words that tell the truth about the way we should live our lives.

Those Bible writers were inspired by God to write words that can surely change our lives for the better.

All of those Bible writers were not brilliant writers.

All of those Bible writers were not highly educated.

Most of the words in the Bible are not big, fancy words that people don't understand.

Most of the words in the Bible are plain and simple words of inspiration written by Bible writers who were inspired by God.

The Bible is the greatest best-seller book, and it has been read from one generation to the next generation by readers and doers of the Bible.

We can truly believe that every word in the Bible is true, even though many writers will write words that are not true.

Jesus Christ, our Lord and savior, is the word of God.

Jesus is the origin of words, and you and I will never run out of words to write about Him, who can always expand our minds with words of inspiration to speak words about Him and write words about Him.

Writing was not always easy for the Bible writers, who had to rely on the holy spirit of God to give them the words to write so that we could all read the truth that sets us free from the devil's lies.

The Bible writers wrote words about the devil for us to read and know that the devil is real and evil, and that he's trying to destroy us.

The Black Voice

The black voice has been speaking out for four hundred years.

That black voice spoke words of bondage with pleas to be set free from slavery.

The white slave owners ignored the black voice for 400 years, but the black voice couldn't keep silent.

The black voice talked about being in chains and shackles down in the old wooden ships that made their way across the ocean waters with very little medical treatment and only a little food to eat.

The black voice talked about being whipped many times for not having enough energy to row the ships so they could reach the sandy beaches on time to meet the new slave owners.

The white slave owners were eager to not hear the black voice telling them that what they were doing was not right.

The white slave owners just didn't want to listen to the black voice that was frightened and vulnerable in the new land where the black voice ended up.

The black voice was purchased by the slave traders in the new land.

The black voice made a loud cry of anguish, disappointment and heartache for the white slave owners to hear, but they just didn't care about setting the black voice free from their white voices enslaving them.

The black voice was told to be quiet and suck it up.

The black voice was wise to not say too much and to not get too tired and weary.

The black voice hummed and sang spiritual songs of freedom in the hot cotton fields where God also heard the black voices sounding so joyful.

The black voice asked God to set them free from slavery one day.

On the quiet nights, the black voice would sound strong in prayer before laying down to sleep.

The black voice would also hear God's voice in their dreams of freedom.

The black voice whispered words of hope in the Underground Railroad as they tried to flee the South and get to the North.

God gave the black voice the power to speak up and speak out against slavery.

God gave the black voice the wisdom to speak out against inequality.

God gave the black voice the knowledge to speak out against segregation.

God gave the black voice the courage to speak out against discrimination.

God gave the black voice the motivation to speak out against injustice.

God gave the black voice the strength to speak out against police brutality.

God fully supports the black voice as it spoke out in love.

God fully supported the black voice when it spoke out in peace.

God fully supported the black voice when it spoke out in joy.

God fully supported the black voice when it spoke out in courage.

God fully supported the black voice when it spoke out in contentment.

God is for the black voice and not against the black voice.

God wanted the black voice to speak up and speak out against prejudice.

God empowered the black voice for thousands of years, going all the way back to Zipporah, the wife of Moses, who Miriam didn't accept because Zipporah wasn't a Hebrew.

God empowered Zipporah to be a strong black woman who didn't let Miriam get her down.

The black voice is still strong today in the news media.

The black voice today is still strong in the church.

The black voice is still strong today in the military.

The black voice is still strong today in protest.

The black voice is still strong today in entertainment.

The black voice is still strong today in sports.

The black voice is still strong today in the home.

The black voice is still strong today in this great nation that the black voice helped to make great.

The black voice is still strong today in the medical field.

The black voice is still strong today in the government.

The black voice is still strong today in science.

The black voice is still strong today in technology.

The black voice is still strong today in the Olympics.

The black voice is still strong today all around the world.

Regardless of the bruises that the black voice got, it couldn't keep the black voice from being heard by God.

Regardless of the sores that the black voice got, it couldn't keep the black voice from being respected by God.

Regardless of the pain that the black voice experienced, it couldn't keep the black voice from being in favor with God.

Regardless of how sick the black voice became, it couldn't keep the black voice from being healed by God.

Regardless of the flaws the black voice had, it never kept the black voice from being blessed by God.

The black voice is a threat to prejudiced people, and the black voice is like a fruit tree to God.

The black voice is a curse to prejudiced people, but the black voice is like good health to God.

The black voice is an enemy to prejudiced people, but the black voice is a friend to God.

The black voice is like a little canoe to prejudiced people, but the black voice is like an aircraft carrier ship to God.

The black voice is the voice of yesterday, today and tomorrow, when the black voice will not keep silent against inhumanity, which is something God will never support.

God greatly supports the black voice.

We Can Mess Things Up

We can mess things up when we truly need the Lord to straighten things out for us.

We can move too fast and mess things up, but we can't blame anybody but ourselves.

We can mess things up and feel so helpless.

We can mess things up and be a disappointment to ourselves.

We can mess things up and not always realize it.

When we mess things up, the Lord is the best one to talk to about what we messed up.

When we mess things up, the Lord is the best one to help us get things right.

When we mess up, no one else can strengthen us like the Lord, who can truly give us the strength to get through what we have messed up.

We can mess up things that can surely cause us to worry.

Only Jesus can truly take away our worry and lift us up with His peace, to be like we hadn't messed up anything at all.

We Need Some Time To

We need some time to rest our minds.

We need some time to relax our bodies.

We need some time to think.

We need some time to sit down.

We need some time to listen.

We need some time to talk.

We need some time to remember.

We need some time to walk.

We need some time to sleep.

We need some time to dream.

We need some time to eat.

We need some time to forgive.

We need some time to cry.

We need some time to grieve.

We need some time to love our enemies.

We need some time to play.

We need some time to agree.

We need some time to come together.

We need some time to get the victory.

We need some time to pray.

We need some time to spend with the Lord.

We need some time to overcome the world.

We need some time to read the Bible.

We need some time to understand the Bible.

We need some time to get to know someone.

We need some time to truly know ourselves.

We need some time to truly know the Lord.

We need some time to get well if we are sick.

We need some time to heal from a broken heart.

We need some time to settle down.

We need some time to grow strong in the Lord.

We need some time to have more faith in the Lord.

We need some time to see people's True Colors.

The Sun Rises and the Sun Sets

The sun rises and the sun sets on the changes that we go through in life that can disarrange our hopes and disarrange our choices.

The sun rises and the sun sets on our existence in the life that the Lord gives to us through the price that He paid for us to live to see this day.

The sun rises and the sun sets on our free will that the Lord gave to us so that we can choose our words to say and choose to do good deeds or evil deeds.

The sun rises and the sun sets on our comings and goings here and there in the land of the living, where only the living are at the mercy and grace of God.

The sun rises in the sun sets on our dreams, goals and reasons to think things through before we make our final decisions to do what is right or do what is wrong.

The sun rises and sets on the saved in Jesus Christ and on those lost in sin.

The Lord ensures that all great and small have a final destiny to face in the end.

A One-Track Mind

There are many church folks who have a one-track mind.

They believe there is only one way to tell people about Jesus Christ.

We can tell people about Jesus in our income.

We can tell people about Jesus in our dreams.

We can tell people about Jesus in our accomplishments.

We can tell people about Jesus in our talents.

We can tell people about Jesus in our skills.

We can tell people about Jesus in our home.

We can tell people about Jesus in our neighborhood.

We can tell people about Jesus in our life experiences.

There are many church folks who have a one-track mind.

They believe that Jesus can only be told about in a sermon.

They believe that Jesus can only be told about in a gospel song.

They believe that Jesus can only be told about in a bible school lesson.

They believe that Jesus can only be told about in a testimony.

They believe that Jesus can only be told about in a poem.

The best way that we can tell people about Jesus Christ is in our body language that can surely tell the truth about you and me.

The Language of Love

The language of love is the best language that we can speak to one another every day.

The language of love is a language that even a fool can understand.

No one in their right mind would complain about the language of love.

No one in their right mind would reject the language of love.

The language of love is a language that many people don't want to speak. The language of love is a language that many people won't except.

The language of love is a language that even animals can understand.

The language of love is a language that even animals can accept.

The language of love is the greatest language to speak every day around the world.

The language of Love Is God, who so loved us first.

The language of love is a language that even an animal would love to speak every day.

Your Time, O Lord

Your time, O Lord, is always on time under the sun that shines on Your time.

My time is not always on time and it makes me look like I'm not worth a dime.

Your time, O Lord, gives me peace of mind all day long, and Your time will not decline.

Your time, O Lord, is so divine in heaven and on earth.

No one can define your time, O Lord, because You are always so kind to help me on Your time.

Your time, O Lord, will never cause me to get left behind like this world's time that will run out one day.

Your time, O Lord, is forever more inclined in your heavenly divine nature.

Many People Believe

Many people believe that there is no God who is beyond their foolish theories that corrupt their hearts.

Many people believe that only feeble-minded people imagine that there is someone high above in the sky

Many people think that God is a figment of weak-minded people's imaginations, no matter who they are and where they live.

Many people believe that especially poor, disturbed people make up more and more tales about an imaginary God who can supply all of their needs.

Many people believe that they are self-made and they believe that we Christians make up imaginary stories about a God for us to worship in this life.

People can believe what they want to believe, but only God is self-made and eternal beyond temporary skeptics who are very odd and abnormal for believing there is no God.

When We Sleep

When we sleep, we don't see anything.

We don't feel anything.

We don't know anything that is going on near us or far away from us.

When we sleep, we can't think about anything.

If we talk in our sleep, we don't know what we said when we wake up.

If we walk in our sleep, we don't know where we are going.

When we sleep, we don't hear anything.

When we sleep, we don't know when we will wake up.

We are not aware of anything.

When we sleep, our mind is blank, and filled with no thoughts.

When we sleep, our hearts are blank and filled with no feelings.

Death is a sleep to the dead who can't say anything.

Death is a sleep to the dead who can't feel anything.

Death is a sleep to the dead, who can't think about anything.

Death is a sleep to the dead who don't know anything.

Death is a sleep to the dead who can't do anything.

Death is a sleep to the dead who can't talk in that sleep.

Death is a sleep to the dead who can't walk in that sleep.

Death is a sleep to the dead, who only Jesus Christ can wake up when He comes back again.

Death is a sleep to the dead, whose bodies will decay and rot to the bone.

It Is Like Leaving the Doors to Our Houses Wide Open

If we don't have faith in Jesus Christ, it is like leaving the doors to our houses wide open to let the insects come in and bite us.

If we reject Jesus Christ, it is like leaving the doors to our houses wide open to let the reptiles come in and bite us.

If we don't love Jesus Christ, it is like leaving the doors to our houses wide open all night long to let the wild animals come in and attack us.

If we don't obey Jesus Christ, it is like leaving the doors to our houses wide open to let the thieves come in and take whatever they want to take away from us.

When it comes to leaving the doors to our hearts wide open, we have no screen porches for our hearts.

Without Jesus being in our hearts, the devil will come in and overpower our hearts with his lies, deceiving you and me.

Our minds and hearts are like doors left wide open for Satan to come in and devour our souls.

We must let Jesus Christ come into our minds and hearts to live our lives unto Him, so He can save us from our sins and give us His spiritual wisdom.

Do We Love Jesus Enough To...

We know that Jesus loves us.

Do we love Jesus enough to not deny Him before others?

We know that Jesus loves us.

Do we love Jesus enough to deny ourselves and pick up our crosses and follow Him?

We know that Jesus loves us.

Do we love Jesus enough to put our trust in Him?

We know that Jesus loves us.

Do we love Jesus enough to believe that He will not fail us?

We know that Jesus loves us.

Do we love Jesus enough to wait on Him to work things out for us?

We know that Jesus loves us.

Do we love Jesus enough to confess and repent of our sins unto Him?

We know that Jesus loves us.

Do we love Jesus enough to keep His Commandments?

God Put His Law in Our Hearts

God put his law in our hearts when we were little children who didn't always obey our parents and felt guilty about it.

God's law in our hearts caused us to feel that guilt even though we didn't know God's law.

No matter how ignorant someone may be, he or she has enough sense to know when something just doesn't seem right because of God's law being in his or her heart.

God's law is righteous and that means that even ignorant people will know when they didn't say something right or do something right.

God put his law in everyone's heart, even though many people today have no knowledge of God's law.

Being ignorant has no power over anyone's free will choice to choose to listen to that righteous inner voice that will also tell a little child to obey his or her parents.

That inner voice is the law of God.

It Will Be Out of This World

It will be out of this world to one day meet all of Your priests, O Lord, when You come back again to receive all of Your righteous children.

It will be out of this world to one day meet all of your prophets walking through the gates of pearls for loving and being you, O Lord.

It will be out of this world to one day meet all of Your disciples who followed You, O Lord, even through the valley of death.

It will be out of this world to one day meet all of Your children, O Lord, who You love and will take to heaven when You come back again.

It will be out of this world for me to meet You, O Lord, on the clouds of glory one day when You will blow your trumpet loud.

It will be out of this world to go with You, O Lord, back to heaven — that will be an experience I will never have in this world until You come back again at the exact time that God the Father will appoint.

And That Is Why You're God

O Lord, there is nothing that You can't do, and that is why you're God, who can do all things.

O Lord, You can make the impossible to be possible, and that is why you're God, who the holy angels sing heavenly songs about forever and ever.

O Lord, You are the creator of all things that will never outdo you, and that is why you're God, who is eternally clever beyond all creatures.

Lord, You can do anything but fail, and that is why you're God, who will one day cast the devil and his demons into hell along with all who are lost for not giving You their hearts.

O Lord, You existed before all things seen and unseen, and that is why you're God, who is love and hope when dreams can crush.

It Is So Easy

It is so easy to get in an accident on the road where we must always pray and ask the Lord to protect us wherever we go.

It is so easy to see what's not good to see, and that is why we must always pray to the Lord to set our eyes free from whatever doesn't need to be in our eyesight.

It is so easy to hear what is not good to hear, and that is why we must always pray to the Lord to lead and guide us to hear what is in His will for us.

It is so easy for our minds to lose focus on the spur of the moment, and that is why we must always pray to the Lord to keep our minds focused on making the right choices every day.

It's Not Easy Being a Christian

It's not easy being a Christian, but I love having faith in Jesus Christ and I can't get enough of loving Him.

It's not easy being a Christian, but I love doing the Lord's holy will that the angels in heaven above will do forever and ever.

It's not easy being a Christian, but I love praying to Jesus Christ who I don't want to ever deny before anyone.

It's not easy being a Christian, but I love treating my neighbor's right, no matter what they have done.

It's not easy being a Christian, but I love holding onto the Lord, even if someone tries to make me look like a liar and doesn't care that the Lord hates a lying tongue.

It's not easy being a Christian, but I love being a Christian and seeing that the Lord loves everyone the same — there is no little me and big you in the Lord's precious eyesight.

Lord, You Wake Me Up

Lord, you wake me up out of my sleep that takes me into the deep unconsciousness where You also dwell to keep me safe.

O Lord, you wake me up out of my dreams that go from one dream to the next, seeming like if it's not one thing it's another thing.

O Lord, you lay me down to sleep in a troubled world and you wake me up in a wide-awakening troubled world.

Lord, you wake me up for me to give you my precious pearls of obedience and trust that the sinners of this world will trample over day after day.

O Lord, you wake me up in the early morning so I can start my day off with thinking of You and giving you my heart, mind, soul and strength that your Holy Angels will guard for making You my choice, when You, O Lord, wake me up.

So Unfair

It was so unfair that my step-daughter died at the young age of 25.

Her mother had also died many years ago.

My step-daughter was like my very own blood daughter when she was alive, and she loved me so dear.

Before my step-daughter died, I didn't understand the grief parents felt when they lost their son or daughter to death.

Her death surely caused me to shed some tears, and I know today what it feels like to lose a child so very dear to my heart.

Her time got out of order on earth through her unfair fate that shortened my step-daughter's precious life.

I could more easily understand this death if my step-daughter had lived a criminal lifestyle that could without a doubt cause her to die at a very young age.

But this was not the case — she was a kind young woman with her hands holding onto good things.

It seemed so unfair that my step-daughter died at a young age.

Her death allowed me to truly see that death is so unfair to everybody, no matter what age we are.

I truly thank God for giving us His Son, Jesus Christ, who is the resurrection to give us eternal life when He comes back again.

No matter how unfair things can be, Jesus is fair and will one day put an end to death and the grave.

An Unpredictable World

We live in an unpredictable world where anything could go wrong at any time, or so it seems.

We live in an unpredictable world where bad things can happen at any time, just like a bad song to sing.

This unpredictable world will get worse and worse with the unpredictability that sin births into this world.

An unpredictable world is where we live from day to day, so we can't put our trust in this world that will pass away one day.

All that we truly have in this unpredictable world is our free will to choose what we do and say for as long as we live.

Like crabs in a barrel pulling down every crab that tries to climb to the top are selfish men, women, boys and girls who will make this unpredictable world more and more wayward from the Lord.

We live in an unpredictable world where no one can predict that there will be a tomorrow for them if the Lord doesn't allow it.

No matter who we are and no matter where we live, this unpredictable world will dig more and more pits of sin for anyone to fall into if they don't live for Jesus Christ, our best friend.

God Wants Us to Love Him

God is love, and God wants us to love Him every day and know that He loves us in every way.

God is the origin of love, and God wants us to love Him.

God is forever more worthy of our love that can never rise above God's love for us.

God gave us a free will choice to love Him or not love Him.

God loved us first when we were in our mothers wombs and didn't know anything.

God is the highest love that we can always trust and His love will never get weak on us.

God wants us to love Him so very much more than anyone else in this world and more than anything in this world.

God wants us to love Him, and He shows His love to all in the land of the living.

God wants us all to love Him, whether we are great or small.

Will Go On

Some things in our lives will go on, even though they are not right, so we must put our trust in the Lord to fight our battles and make things right for us.

Some things in the church will go on, even though they're not right, so we must ask the Lord to keep us strong in His might and power so He can keep us from falling down in living in sin.

Some things will go on in our minds that are not right, so we must think on the Lord who we should never deny in our minds because the Lord knows all of our thoughts.

Some things will go on in our hearts that are not right, and only the Lord can keep our hearts from getting caught up in selfishness if we love Him every day and every night.

Some things in our free will will go on that are not right, and we need to pray to the Lord to help us make good choices in our lives because we can say something wrong and do something wrong on the spur of the moment.

The Mind

The mind can be strong.

The mind can be weak.

The mind can be great.

The mine can be wise.

The mind can be foolish.

The mind can be well.

The mind can be sick.

The mind can be intelligent.

That mind can be brilliant.

The mind can be genius.

The mind can be troubled.

The mind can be sound.

The mind can be insecure.

The mind can change.

The mind can be powerful if the mind is at peace with Jesus Christ.

The mind is renewed in Jesus Christ.

The mind can be right.

The mind can be wrong.

The mind can be good.

The mind can be evil.

The mind can be carnal.

The mind is spiritual in Jesus Christ.

The mind can be in bondage.

The mind is free in Jesus Christ.

The mind can be settled.

The mind can be hasty.

The mind can be brainwashed.

The mind can be beautiful.

The mind can be ugly.

The mind can be prepared.

The mind can be unrealistic.

The mind can be filthy.

The mind can be sinful.

The mind that stays on Jesus Christ is a holy and righteous mind.

The mind that stays on Jesus Christ is a realistic mind, because Jesus is forevermore real than whatever we see, hear, taste, tough and feel.

The mind can be simple.

The mind can be corrupt.

The mind can be immoral.

The mind can be moral.

The mind is victorious in Jesus Christ.

The mind will overcome the world in Jesus Christ.

The mind is secured in Jesus Christ.

The mind can be confused.

The mind can be deep.

The mind can be sincere.

The mind can be insincere.

The mind can be weary.

The mind can be greedy.

The mind can be unstable.

The mind that stays on Jesus Christ is a content mind.

You and I Can Deny Jesus

You and I can deny Jesus, when He gives us the opportunity to speak His holy name before strangers.

You and I can deny Jesus in the way that we dress.

You and I can deny Jesus by what we eat. You and I can deny Jesus by what we drink.

You and I can deny Jesus and not even realize it.

You and I can deny Jesus in more than one way.

You and I can deny Jesus like Peter did.

Peter was one of Jesus's disciples who denied Jesus three times.

You and I can deny Jesus by our actions.

You and I can deny Jesus by what we say.

You and I can deny Jesus in some kind of way on any day.

If we deny ourselves we can't deny Jesus.

We can easily let ourselves get in the way of Jesus.

You and I can easily deny Jesus in our homes.

You and I can easily deny Jesus in our communities.

You and I can easily deny Jesus, even in the church.

We must deny ourselves and pick up our crosses and follow Jesus Christ.

If you and I don't deny ourselves, we deny Jesus.

To deny ourselves is to put Jesus first in our lives every day.

It's a Miracle to Me

It's a miracle to me, O Lord, that You can use a messed-up person like me.

I know, O Lord, that I don't deserve to be used by You.

I know that all of my righteousness is like filthy rags to you, O Lord, when I can believe that my righteousness is so good in my eyes.

Who am I to believe that I deserve You, O Lord, to answer my prayers.

It's a miracle to me, O Lord, that you brought me this far when some of my loved ones have departed from the land of the living.

I truly deserve to be in the grave that You, O Lord, saved me from so I could see this day.

O Lord, who am I to ever take You for granted in any kind of way.

It's a miracle to me, O Lord, that you see who I can become in Your holy and righteous name.

O Lord, I don't want to do my will because that will surely make me selfish, but Your holy will is freedom and sets me free from my own will that will put me in bondage every day.

It's a miracle to me, O Lord, that You still love me when I don't always love You or trust You to always be there for me.

I know, O Lord, that I am guilty of doubting that You will bring me through what I can't bring myself through.

It's a miracle to me, O Lord, that You never gave up on me when I had given up on You to chase behind this world that greatly disappointed me when I caught up with it.

It's a miracle to me, O Lord, that You didn't allow the devil to destroy me in my sins when I turned my back on You.

O Lord, There is Nothing

O Lord, there is nothing that You don't know how to do.

O Lord, there is nothing that You don't know how to say.

O Lord, there is nothing that You don't know what to say.

O Lord, there is nothing that You can't do.

O Lord, there is no place where You can't go.

O Lord, there is nothing that can rise above You.

O Lord, there is nothing that can get ahead of You.

O Lord, there is nothing that can keep up with You.

O Lord, there is nothing that can get the best of You.

O Lord, there is nothing that can get You down.

O Lord, there is nothing that can pass by You.

O Lord, there is nothing that can get around You.

O Lord, there is nothing that can stop You from doing what You want to do.

O Lord, there is nothing that You can't defeat.

O Lord, there is nothing that You can't understand.

O Lord, there is nothing that can't be changed by You.

O Lord, there is nothing that You can't see.

Oh Lord there is nothing that You can't hear.

O Lord, there is nothing that You can't feel.

O Lord, there is nothing that You don't know.

O Lord, there is nothing impossible to You.

O Lord, there is nothing new to You.

O Lord, there is nothing bad in You.

O Lord, there is nothing unstable in You.

O Lord, there is nothing lawless in You.

O Lord, there is nothing imperfect in You.

O Lord, there is nothing wrong with You.

O Lord, there is nothing boring about You.

O Lord, there is nothing unfair about You.

O Lord, there is nothing powerless about You.

O Lord, there is nothing fearful about You.

O Lord, there is nothing unreasonable about You.

O Lord, there is nothing that You can't fix.

O Lord, there is nothing too hard for You.

O Lord, there is nothing that You can't solve.

O Lord, there is nothing that You can't get rid of.

O Lord, there is nothing that You can't predict.

O Lord, there is nothing that You can't be precise about.

O Lord, there is nothing that can be too big for You.

O Lord, there is nothing that You can't check out.

O Lord, there is nothing that You can't restore.

O Lord, there is nothing that You can't conquer.

O Lord, there is nothing that You can't open up.

O Lord, there is nothing that You can't close out.

O Lord, there is nothing that You can't rule over.

O Lord, there is nothing that You can't answer.

O Lord, there is nothing that You can't decide.

O Lord, there is nothing that You can't fulfill.

O Lord, there is nothing that You can't straighten out.

O Lord, there is nothing that You can't work out.

O Lord, there is nothing that You can't move out of anyone's way.

O Lord, there is nothing that You can't build.

O Lord, there is nothing that You can't knock down.

O Lord, there is nothing that You can't walk by.

O Lord, there is nothing that You can't step over.

O Lord, there is nothing that You can't start.

O Lord,, there is nothing that You can't finish.

O Lord, there is nothing that You can't reveal.

O Lord, there is nothing that You can't make sure.

O Lord, there is nothing that You can't cleanse.

O Lord, there is nothing that You can't say.

O Lord, there is nothing that You can't make new.

O Lord, there is nothing that You can't find.

O Lord, there is nothing that you can't recover.

O Lord, there is nothing that You can't set free.

O Lord, there is nothing that You can't cure.

O Lord, there is nothing that You can't make real.

A Wake-Up Call

The Lord is giving this whole world a wake-up call in the form of the coronavirus that has killed over a million people.

The Lord is trying to wake us up out of our spiritual deep sleep because this world will get no better.
The Lord Jesus Christ is coming back again one day soon, and He is sounding the alarm to all the world.

We are living in these last days of troubled times and we can't afford to overlook this when our soul's salvation is on the line.

We need to confess and repent of all of our sins unto the Lord Jesus Christ.

The Lord is giving us a final wake-up call so that we can dedicate our lives unto Him before it's too late.

We don't know when our day will come to take us to the world of the dead.

The grave is already filled with countless dead people from way back in the Bible days up until today.

The Lord has given this world a wake-up call to turn away from living by eyesight and start living by faith in Him.

Time is getting tired of waiting on people who love to make excuses for their sins.

The Lord is giving this world a wake-up call so that everyone can see that this world is very weary and ready to give up on hope.

The Lord is giving this world a wake-up call so everyone can see that this world will fail everybody.

We can't put our trust in anything in this world, because it will one day pass away.

The Lord is giving this world a wake-up call, because time is getting shorter and shorter and will very soon run out on this whole world.

The Lord doesn't want anyone to be lost in sin, but so many people will be lost for not believing in Jesus Christ.

So many people are spiritually asleep and don't want to wake up to the Lord's call of salvation that's given to all men, women, boys and girls.

There are many church folks who are spiritually awake but will fall spiritually asleep when their faith is tested.

There are many church folks who are spiritually awake but will fall spiritually asleep when their trials knock them down on the hard rocks of what looks impossible to them.

All around this world, many people can see that things are in a big mess.

All around this world, many people can see that this world is in bondage to natural disasters.

All around this world, many people can see that so many things are not right.

The Lord is giving this whole world a wake-up call, whether people are educated or uneducated.

The Lord is giving this world a wake-up call, whether people are rich or poor, good or bad.

Everybody in this world is eligible for a wake-up call from the Lord, who loves everybody in this world.

We are living in the last days in this world, which will come to an end when we least expect it.

We church folks know about the Lord's wake-up call for us and we are going to be held accountable for not letting the world know that it's time to spiritually wake up and repent and turn to the Lord God before it's too late.

Love Falls in Love

Love falls in love with love that will sooner or later blow the cover off of people who pretend to love you and me.

Love falls in love with fair people who love to treat everyone fairly.

There is no fairness in pretense love that will mistreat true love every day.

Pretending people will use their pretense love to fool you and me into believing that they love us.

Love falls in love with innocent people.

Many people have fallen in love with someone that they believed to love them, when they only pretended to love them.

Love falls in love with love because love is very appealing to so many people.

Love falls in love with honest people who love to tell the truth in love.

Love falls in love with humble people.

Love falls in love with loving people who love people of every race, creed and culture.

Pretense love will truly fool you and me if we don't love Jesus Christ with all of our minds, hearts, souls and strength.

Love falls in love with people who love equality.

Love falls in love with people who love peace and order.

Love falls in love with people who love unity.

Love falls in love with people who love justice.

Love falls in love with people who love freedom.

Love falls in love with people who especially love the Lord Jesus Christ.

Love falls in love with God at first sight, because if there is no God, there is no love.

God so loved us first when pretense love can never cause God's love to fail you and me.

Love is the greatest feeling in this world.

Even a person who pretends to love wants to feel love from people so that they can be sure to get what they want from them.

Pretending people love to pretend to love people because doing that can help them get worldly gain.

Love falls in love with love that hates sin, but loves the sinner who Jesus loves to save from being lost in sin.

Pretense love is no love to fall in love with love.

Pretense love is from the devil, who is the greatest pretender.

The devil cannot fool the Lord with his pretense love.

Love will sooner or later show you the truth about the people who truly love you.

We Are Not Perfect Without Sin

We will not say the right words all of the time.

We will not do the right things all the time.

We are not perfect.

We all will make some mistakes.

We all have some bad habits.

We will not think right all of the time.

The best Christians in the world are not perfect without sins to confess and repent unto the Lord Jesus Christ.

We all will fall short of the glory of God because we were born in sin.

Even though we are not perfect without sin, it doesn't mean that we have to live in our sins.

We can choose not to live in our sins by living right unto the Lord.

We can choose to confess all of our sins and live a renewed life doing the Lord's will.

God's will is perfect for you and me and will make us want to live a holy life and righteous life unto the Lord, who is perfect without sin.

Through the Lord's perfection, we can come to Him boldly and ask Him to help us to be who He wants us to be in His holy name.

We are not perfect without sin, but the Lord can give us the strength to resist the devil's temptation from overtaking us and making us sin against Him.

Even the best Christians can sin against the Lord, and they may not know that they have sinned because there are seen sins and unseen sins.

We can commit a sin that we don't even see right away until the Lord opens our eyes and shows us that unseen sin we committed against Him.

We can truly thank the Lord Jesus Christ for giving up His life on the cross to save us from our sins.

We don't have to live in our sins and we don't have to die in our sins because of Jesus Christ, who overcame the world.

All of the prophets and priests in the Bible we're not perfect without sin.

They had sins to confess and repent of unto God.

They all had fallen short of the glory of God.

The prophets and priests had to make an atonement for their sins.

The prophets and priests didn't always put all of their trust in God, and by doing that they had sinned against God.

We are not perfect without sin and that is why we must come to Jesus and ask Him to forgive us of our sins.

Only Jesus Christ was perfect without sin when he lived on earth among us sinners.

We can sin against God in our thoughts, even before we say one word.

We can sin against God in our thoughts, even before we do anything.

We can sin against God even before we think it.

Sin can travel faster than the speed of sound.

Sin can travel faster than the speed of light.

The devil's temptations can be faster than the speed of light.

We can easily believe that sin can only creep up on us, but sin can be so quick that it can even take our life in a split second.

We are not perfect without sin, but Jesus became our sins on the cross in our place.

Jesus rose from the grave with victory over the grave and death that comes from sin.

I Have Nothing to Complain About

I have nothing to complain about when there are people who are blind and can't see.

I have nothing to complain about when there are people who can›t hear anything.

I have nothing to complain about when there are people who have no arms and hands.

I have nothing to complain about when there are people who are paralyzed.

I have nothing to complain about when there are people who have no legs.

I have nothing to complain about when there are people who have no feet.

I have nothing to complain about when there are people who have no houses to live in.

I have nothing to complain about when there are people who have no cars to drive.

I have nothing to complain about when there are people who have no jobs.

I have nothing to complain about when there are people who can't breathe on their own.

I have nothing to complain about when there are people who have lost their businesses.

I have nothing to complain about when there are people who have lost their minds.

I have nothing to complain about when there are people who have lost everything they owned.

I have nothing to complain about when there are people who have taken their own lives.

I have nothing to complain about when there are people who have lost their memories.

I have nothing to complain about when there are people who can't talk.

I have nothing to complain about when there are people whose dreams have been crushed.

I have nothing to complain about when there are people who have been abused and haven't been healed.

I have nothing to complain about when there are people who have lost loved ones and can't move on.

I have nothing to complain about when there are people who have no food to eat.

I have nothing to complain about when there are people who have no clean water to drink.

I have nothing to complain about when there are people who are dying right now.

I have nothing to complain about when there are people who can tell me that I have it good.

I have nothing to complain about when there are people who can tell me that I am rich.

I have nothing to complain about when there are people who can tell me that I'm not going through much of anything at all.

I have nothing to complain about when there are people who can tell me that I have nothing to complain about.

Complaining cannot solve problems.

Complaining can make problems much worse.

Complaining can cause your blood pressure to go up.

Complaining can cause us to not get a good night's sleep.

Complaining can cause us to get weary.

Complaining will make us feel discontent.

Complaining will cause us to not put our trust in the Lord.

Complaining will cause us to displease the Lord.

Complaining can cause us to not have faith in the Lord.

Complaining can call us to stray away from the Lord.

Complaining has caused many marriages to fail.

Complaining is of the devil who complained about God to the angels in heaven.

I have nothing to complain about when I don't deserve to be alive today that the Lord is my hope, and I am thankful unto Him for bringing me this far in my life.

The Truth

It is always good to tell the truth, because doing that will set us free from lies.

Telling the truth is what the Lord wants us to do every day.

Telling the truth is what the Lord requires us to do every day.

A liar hates to tell the truth.

A liar will not tell the truth.

The truth can sometimes hurt us, but the truth will set us free from lies.

It's much better for the truth to hurt us than to be hurt by a lie.

We should love to tell the truth every day.

An honest judge and jury loves to hear the truth in the courtroom.

A husband loves for his wife to tell him the truth.

A wife loves for her husband to tell her the truth.

Parent's love for their children to tell them the truth.

We love for our friends to tell us the truth.

We love for our neighbors to tell us the truth.

We can always believe the bible to tell us the truth.

We can always trust the Lord to be the Living Truth.

We love for our state and government leaders to tell us the truth.

The truth in this world is in the minority party.

The lies in this world are in the majority party.

So many people in this world will believe a lie over the truth.

So many people in this world would rather live a lie than to live the truth of God's holy word.

God will not let anyone get away with telling lies.

God is against living a lie every day.

When has the truth ever caused anyone to regret living the truth of God's holy word?

We can regret telling a lie, and we can regret living a lie.

The truth is eternal in Jesus Christ, who cannot lie.

The truth is eternal in God, who cannot lie, just like His son Jesus Christ.

The truth is eternal in God's holy word that was written by holy men inspired by the Holy Spirit, who cannot lie.

The devil is a liar every day.

He tells his lies to you and me in so many different ways.

If we don't know God's holy word, we can so easily believe the devil's lies that will surely sooner or later wreck our lives.

When has the truth of God's holy word ever wrecked anyone's life?

When has Jesus Christ ever wrecked anyone's life?

The truth is Jesus Christ, who gives us an abundance of life for believing in Him who is the truth over every lie.

Don't Keep Jesus on the Cross

Don't keep Jesus on the cross when Jesus is up in heaven making our pleas before God.

Jesus got the victory over death and the grave.

Jesus Christ, our Lord, is the resurrection beyond the cross that Jesus overcame with eternal life to give to you and me if we are saved in Him.

Don't keep Jesus on the cross as if you can't pray to Him and ask Him to forgive you of your sins.

The cross will always remind us that Jesus laid down His life for our sins.

The cross will always remind us that Jesus suffered and bled on the cross in our place.

Many people will keep Jesus on the cross, believing that Jesus can't give them the power to live a Christian Life.

Jesus has gone beyond the cross that He hung on when He said to God, "Forgive them for they do not know what they do."

Don't keep Jesus on the cross as if Jesus is still nailed to the cross that He got the victory over.

We must live our Christian lives like Jesus has got the victory over our sins.

We must live our Christian lives like Jesus is no longer on the cross.

Jesus has given us the victory over the cross so that we can deny ourselves and pick up our crosses and follow Him to heaven, where there will be no cross for us to bear.

When we see Jesus in heaven, we will see His nail prints in His hands and feet.

Don't keep Jesus on the cross because that was for only a moment so God could see His Son nailed to the cross as He was saving all men from their sins.

We shouldn't keep Jesus on the cross as if He is still suffering and bleeding for our sins.

Don't keep Jesus on the cross because He could have come down off that cross and turned His back on all the world, leaving us lost in sin that could not keep Him on the cross.

What Kind of Clothes Do We Wear?

Do we wear clean clothes of righteousness?

Do we wear clean clothes of holiness?

Do we wear clean clothes of obedience unto the Lord?

Do we wear clean clothes of love?

Do we wear dirty clothes of lust?

Do we wear dirty clothes of greed?

Do we wear dirty clothes of discontentment?

Do we wear dirty clothes of jealousy?

Do we wear dirty clothes of strife?

Do we wear clean clothes of peace?

Do we wear clean clothes of joy?

Do we wear clean clothes of temperance?

Do we wear clean clothes of kindness?

Do we wear clean clothes of gentleness?

Do we wear dirty clothes of prejudice?

Do we wear dirty clothes of Injustice?

Do we wear dirty clothes of hatred?

Do we wear dirty clothes and violence?

What kind of clothes do we put on to wear every day?

Do we wear clean clothes of justice?

Do we wear clean clothes of humility?

Do we wear clean clothes of selflessness?

Do we wear dirty clothes of selfishness?

Do we wear dirty clothes of pride?

Who wants to walk around naked with no clothes on every day?

Even a foolish person will put on some clothes to wear.

Do we wear the dirty clothes of rebelliousness against God?

Do we wear the clean clothes of reverence unto God?

Do we know what kind of clothes we wear every day?

Do we wear clean clothes of telling the truth?

Do we wear dirty clothes of telling lies?

Do we wear clean clothes of faith in the Lord?

Do we wear dirty clothes of playing church?

The clothes that we wear can get some attention.

The clothes that we wear can comfort us.

The clothes that we wear can decrease our image.

The clothes that we wear can heighten our image.

The clothes that we wear can reveal who we are.

Every day, we wear our material clothes to cover up our naked bodies.

We can choose what color of clothes we want to wear.

We can choose to wear clean clothes or dirty clothes day after day.

If we are wise, we will wear the spiritually clean clothes of the Lord Jesus Christ.

Will Get Jealous of You

Some people will get jealous of you if you look better than them.

Some people will get jealous of you if you are smarter than them.

Some people will get jealous of you if you have a better job than them.

Some people will get jealous of you if you make more money than them.

Some people will get jealous of you if you dress better than them.

Some people will get jealous of you if you talk better than them.

Some people will get jealous of you if your house looks better than their house.

Some people will get jealous of you if your car looks better than their car.

Some people will get jealous of you if your truck looks better than their truck.

People will get jealous of you if you are a better athlete than them.

Some people will get jealous of you if you work better than them.

Some people will get jealous of you if you have more friends than them.

Some people will get jealous of you if you are more educated than them.

Some people will get jealous of you if you sing better than them.

Some people will get jealous of you if you get more attention than they do.

Some people will get jealous of you if you are more successful than them.

Some church folks will get jealous of you if you have more spiritual gifts than they do.

Some church folks will get jealous of you if you can pray better than they do.

Some church folks will get jealous of you if you can teach Bible school lessons better than them.

Some church folks will get jealous of you if you can preach better than them.

Some church folks will get jealous of you if you give God the glory and praise Him more than them.

Some church folks will get jealous of you if you have more Bible knowledge than they do.

Some church folks will get jealous of you if you are thankful unto the Lord more than they are.

Some church folks will get jealous of you if you are more faithful unto the Lord then them.

Some church folks will get jealous of you if you are more obedient unto the Lord than they are.

Some church folks will get jealous of you if you go to church more than they do.

Some church folks will get jealous of you if your ministry is more effective than their ministry.

The devil will get jealous of you for believing in Jesus Christ, who the devil rebelled against up in heaven.

The devil will get jealous of you for being saved in Jesus Christ, when the devil is lost forever in his sins and has no chance to live in Heaven again.

The devil is jealous of you and me because we have a chance to make it into heaven through Jesus Christ.

If God Gives You a Gift

If God gives you a gift to be a pilot, then no one can take that away from you.

If God gives you a gift to be a judge, then no one can take that away from you.

If God gives you a gift to be a surgeon, then no one can take that away from you.

If God gives you a gift to be a publisher, then no one can take that away from you.

If God gives you a gift to be a writer, then no one can take that away from you.

If God gives you a gift to be a doctor, then no one can take that away from you.

If God gives you a gift to be a nurse, then no one can take that away from you.

If God gives you a gift to be a news reporter, then no one can take that away from you.

If God gives you a gift to be an engineer, then no one can take that away from you.

If God gives you a gift to be a social worker, then no one can take that away from you.

If God gives you a gift to be a psychologist, then no one can take that away from you.

If God gives you a gift to be a psychiatrist, then no one can take that away from you.

If God gives you a gift to be a teacher, then no one can take that away from you.

If God gives you a gift to be a preacher, then no one can take that away from you.

If God gives you a gift to be a lawyer, then no one can take that away from you.

If God gives you a gift to be a politician, then no one can take that away from you.

If God gives you a gift to sing, then no one can take that away from you.

If God gives you a gift to build houses, then no one can take that away from you.

If God gives you a gift to drive tractor trailer trucks, then no one can take that away from you

If God gives you a gift to be a police officer, then no one can take that away from you.

If God gives you a gift to be a firefighter, then no one can take that away from you.

If God gives you a gift to be an athlete, then no one can take that away from you.

If God gives you a gift to talk, then no one can take that away from you.

If God gives you a gift to listen, then no you can take that away from me.

If God gives you a gift to heal, then no one can take that away from you.

If God gives you the gift of wisdom, then no one can take that away from me.

If God gives you the gift of knowledge, then no one can take that away from you.

If God gives you the gift to make a lot of money, then no one can take that away from you.

If God gives you the gift to help people, and no one can take that away from you.

If God gives you the gift to understand people, then no one can take that away from you.

If God gives you the gift to make people laugh, then no one can take that away from you.

If God gives you the gift to be an actor, then no one can take that away from you.

If God gives you a gift to encourage people, then no one can take that away from you.

If God gives you a gift to motivate people, then no one can take that away from you.

If God gives you a gift to be a mechanic, then no one can take that away from you.

If God gives you a gift to be a poet, then no one can take that away from you.

If God gives you a gift to be a hairstylist, then no one can take that away from you.

If God gives you a gift to speak different languages, then no one can take that away from you.

If God gives you a gift to smile, then no one can take that away from you.

Whatever gifts that God gives to you and me, no one can take them away from us.

You and I can take away our own gifts if we don't use our gifts for the Lord.

You And I Can't Always Tell

You and I can't always tell if someone likes us or doesn't like us.

You and I can't always tell if someone loves us or doesn't love us.

You and I can't always tell if someone is jealous of us or not jealous of us.

You and I can't always tell if someone likes talking to us or doesn't like talking to us.

You and I can't always tell if we are welcome in someone's house or not welcome in someone's house.

You and I can't always tell if someone is telling us the truth or lying to us.

You and I can't always tell if someone is real with us or not real with us.

You and I can't always tell if someone is a phony or is not a phone.

You and I can't always tell if someone is happy for us or not happy for us.

You and I can't always tell if someone is on our side or not on our side.

You and I can't always tell if someone is happy to see us or is not happy to see us.

You and I can't always tell if someone is a Christian or not a Christian.

You and I can't always tell if someone is good or bad.

You and I can't always tell if someone is for us or against us.

You and I can't always tell if someone is our enemy or is not our enemy.

You and I can't always tell if we will make the right choice.

You and I can't always tell if we will say the right word.

You and I can't always tell if someone will help us or not help us.

You and I can't always tell whether someone will let us down or not let us down.

You and I can't always tell if someone wants the best for us or doesn't want the best for us.

Only the Lord knows the heart that always tells the truth about everyone.

Only the Lord knows the heart that always tells the truth about our motives and intentions.

You and I can't always tell if someone's motives are true or not true.

You and I can't always tell if someone's intentions are true or not true.

You and I can't always tell if someone's faith is strong in the Lord or not strong in the Lord.

You and I can't always tell if our faith is strong in the Lord when our trials can surely let us know how strong our faith in the Lord is.

History

We can't erase the bad things that happened in history.

History has so much to do with what is going on in this world today.

History has a lot of power over our lives today.

History has a bad effect on some people today.

History is not a good thing for so many people today.

The bad things that happened in history have caused many people to be angry today.

The bad things that happened in history have caused many people to be sad today.

The bad things that happened in history have caused many people to be hurt today.

There is good history for many people, who believe that what happened in history is a good thing.

The Bible is filled with history for you and me to read about today.

Enoch, Moses, Elijah and Jesus Christ are not history today because they are alive up in heaven, while everyone else in the Bible is in the grave and is history today.

One day you and I will be history if we die before Jesus Christ comes back again.

History is not all bad, when it's the good history that spearheads this nation to be great today.

History is not all bad, when it's the good history that gives many people hope today.

History is not all bad, when it's the good history that gives many people joy today.

Good history has the victory over bad history, when many people will only talk about the bad history.

There is some good history in every race, creed and culture of people.

There is some bad history in every race, creed and culture of people.

No one can erase history, no matter whether the history is good or bad.

We can surely thank God for the good history, even though the bad history has caused many people to be broken up in pain today.

Good history will always be around us like the air that we breathe, but God is our strength so that we can bear the bad history.

Making Choices
is a Serious Thing

Making choices is a serious thing every day, and many people don't believe that their choices are serious things.

Making good choices has a good effect on so many people.

Making bad choices has a bad effect on so many people.

Making good choices will show and tell that you are a good person.

Making bad choices will show and tell that you are a bad person.

We all will make our choices to do what we want to do, whether we make good choices or bad choices.

The choices that you and I make will have a good or bad effect on other people in our family.

The choices that you and I make will have a good or bad effect on our friends.

The choices that you and I make will have a good or bad effect on our neighbors.

The choices that you and I make will have a good or bad effect on ourselves.

Making choices is a serious thing, even though many people make them out to be a joke.

Making choices is a serious thing that many people take too lightly.

Making choices is a serious thing that so many people couldn't care less about.

You and I will become the choices that we make, and other people will see this sooner or later.

You and I will become the choices we make, and will see that sooner or later too.

No one can hide from their choices.

Choices are so transparent every day.

Making choices is a serious thing that so many people overlook and consider to be nothing.

Making choices is always a serious thing to God, who gave us all the free will to make our own choices, whether they are good or bad choices.

If you want to know what kind of person someone is, just look at the choices that he or she makes.

If you want to know what kind of person you are, just look at the choices that you make.

My choices and your choices will define who we are everyday.

Making choices is a serious thing, and the Lord did not create us to be robots to do whatever he wants us to do.

God gave us a free will to choose to say what we want to say and to choose to do what we want to do, whether it be right or wrong.

God gave us all a free will to choose to love and obey him or to not love and obey him. We will pay the cost for the choices that we make, and the devil cannot force us to make bad choices.

The devil can only tempt us to make bad choices, and we can choose not to make those bad choices.

Many people will say that the devil made them do this or that.

The devil can't take away our free will that God gave to us to choose from right from wrong.

The devil can't take away our free will that God gave to us to choose good or evil.

Our choices that we make is on us, and God will hold us accountable.

Making choices is a serious thing every day, and our choices are like our shadows that will follow us around wherever we go.

Making good choices will sooner or later pay off real good for us.

Making choices is a serious thing but many people won't accept that it is serious.

God sees every choice that you and I make, and God takes them seriously.

Our Soul's salvation is at stake by the choices that we make.

We human beings are the only ones who can make choices on Earth.

No other creature has a free will to make choices.

We human beings have no excuses before God to believe that we can't do what is right in this world.

Even children have a free will to choose to learn how to obey their parents.

If children couldn't choose how to obey their parents, then God would not have made it a commandment for children to obey their parents.

The same commandment applies to grown-up children to keep, as long as their parents are telling them what is good for them in the eyes of God.

Making choices is a serious thing, and no matter how brilliant you are you can make some bad choices.

No matter how sure you are, you can make some bad choices that can ruin your good name.

No matter how careful you are, you can make some bad choices.

No matter how religious you are, you can make some bad choices.

No one is exempt from making bad choices.

No one is exempt from making good choices.

Thanks to the good Lord, we have a free will to choose that the devil can't take away from us.

Making choices is a serious thing, but so many people don't believe that.

Making choices is always a serious thing to God who loves for us to make good choices every day.

Making good choices can surely save many lives.

Making good choices can surely prosper you and me.

Making good choices can give you and me a good day.

Making good choices will make this world a better place to live in.

Making choices is a serious thing, and making bad choices will sooner or later make us regret it.

Whoever doesn't have any regrets for making bad choices is a fool, especially in the eyes of God.

Making choices is a serious thing that we all need to take seriously

We should not take our free will choices for granted, because that is not pleasing to God.

The Greatest Deception

The greatest deception is to deceive yourself into believing that you are someone you are not.

To deceive yourself is wanting to be worshipped instead of worshipping God.

Lucifer deceived himself and wanted to be worshipped above God.

To deceive ourselves is wanting to be lord over the flock in the church.

There is only one Lord Jesus Christ, who is the head of the church.

To deceive ourselves is to believe that we are perfect without any sins to confess and repent of.

Only Jesus Christ was perfect without any sins to confess and repent of.

The greatest deception is to deceive ourselves into believing that we are always right about what we say.

The greatest deception is to deceive yourself into believing that you are always right about what you do.

To deceive yourself is to believe that you can say nothing wrong.

To deceive yourself is to believe that you can do nothing wrong.

To deceive yourself is to make excuses for your sins.

To deceive yourself is to not believe that you are a sinner.

To deceive yourself is to believe that you don't have to keep God's Commandments.

To deceive yourself is to believe that you can live in your sins and still go to heaven.

The greatest deception is to deceive yourself into thinking you are holy when you're living your life being of the world.

To deceive yourself is to believe that you are good when you're doing bad things.

To deceive yourself is to believe that you know everything, when even a child can ask you a question that you may not have the answer to.

The greatest deception is to deceive yourself into believing what Lucifer believed up in heaven where he was cast out of for trying to exalt himself above God for believing that he could be God.

To deceive yourself is to believe that your good works can save you.

To deceive yourself is to believe that you can live your life any kind of way and still be saved.

To deceive yourself is to believe that you are self-made, when the Lord made it possible for you to be successful today.

The greatest deception is to deceive yourself to believe that you can do all things, when the Lord may give you a simple thing that you can fail to do.

To deceive yourself is the greatest deception that Lucifer and the fallen angels truly know, because they fear and tremble before the Lord who cast them out of Heaven.

To deceive yourself is to believe that there is no God.

To deceive yourself is to believe that you can die and go to heaven without Jesus Christ coming back again to take you there if you are saved in Him.

To deceive yourself is to believe that you own your body and can do as you please with it, when your body is Jesus' Holy Temple that He owns every day.

To deceive yourself is to believe that you love God, who you don't see, but hate your neighbor who you do see.

The greatest deception is to believe that you are a Christian while not going through any suffering for Jesus' name sake.

The greatest deception is to deceive yourself into believing that you are innocent when you are guilty.

To deceive yourself is to believe that you made the right choice, when you made the wrong choice.

To deceive yourself is to believe that you are strong, when you are weak.

The greatest deception is to believe that you are God who cannot lie, when you are lying to yourself because you believe that you are God.

To deceive yourself is to believe that you love Jesus Christ, while you don't keep all of His Ten Commandments.

To deceive yourself is to believe that you won't reap what you sow.

To deceive yourself is to believe that what you say and do won't have an effect on others.

The greatest deception is to deceive yourself into believing that you are God's most favored one in the church body of Jesus Christ, when the church body has many members that Jesus favors all the same to build up His church.

No one member is more favored than another member in the eyes of God.

The greatest deception is to deceive yourself into believing that you are living a moral life, when you are not living your life unto the Lord who is eternally moral.

The greatest deception is to deceive ourselves into believing that we can say bad words to others and do bad things to others and get away with it.

The Lord says that we will reap what we sow, for sooner or later we will get back what we dish out to others.

We may not get it back in the exact same way, but we will get it back in some kind of way.

The greatest deception is to deceive ourselves into believing that we are saved in Jesus Christ and that we don't have to go through any hardships for Jesus' holy name sake.

The greatest deception is to deceive ourselves that we are only human to give in to the devil's temptations that Jesus overcame and can give you and me the power to resist if we live our lives unto Him.

Jesus is our divine Lord and Savior who took on our humanity to give us the power to take on His divine nature that is unlimited to us for believing in Jesus Christ.

The greatest deception is to deceive ourselves into believing that we are true to ourselves and don't have to be true to Jesus, who is the truth to set us free from anything that's not like Him.

Caught Up

We can't be caught up in Jesus Christ and be caught up in the world at the same time.

Either we are all for Jesus or we are all for the world.

Being caught up in Jesus is staying in prayer without ceasing.

Being caught up in Jesus is loving Him and obeying Him every day.

Being caught up in Jesus is reading His holy word every day.

Being caught up in Jesus is loving our neighbors every day.

Being caught up in Jesus as being humble unto Him every day.

Being caught up in Jesus is denying ourselves and putting Jesus above ourselves every day.

Being caught up in Jesus is not being a friend to this world.

Being caught up in Jesus is keeping our faith in Jesus every day.

Being caught up in Jesus is knowing that Jesus will supply all of our needs.

Being caught up in Jesus is being willing to die for His holy name's sake.

Being caught up in Jesus is believing that Jesus is coming back again.

So many people are caught up in this world.

They put their trust in this world.

They live to please this world.

They don't put their trust in Jesus Christ.

They don't live to please Jesus Christ.

So many people are caught up in the things in this world.

They live for pleasure.

They live for thrills.

They live for money.

They live for power.

They live for their appetites.

They live for sex.

They live for greed.

They live for recognition.

They live for fame.

They live for corruption.

They live for lawlessness.

We can't be caught up in Jesus Christ and be caught up in this world at the same time.

The best thing that anyone can do is to be caught up in Jesus Christ.

Many people want to go to heaven, but they don't want to be caught up in Jesus Christ, who created the heavens and the Earth.

Being caught up in Jesus Christ will give us strength and comfort us when trouble comes our way.

Being caught up in Jesus Christ is heaven on Earth.

Being caught up in this world and thinking it's like heaven is bad for many people, because this world will fail and all who are caught up in it will be left behind to wake up in the second resurrection.

We Can't Rush the Lord

We can't rush the Lord to answer our prayers on our time.

We must wait on the Lord to answer our prayers in His time that is always on time.

We can't rush the Lord to open a door for us when that door may have been shut for a long time because the Lord wanted it to be shut for a long time.

We can't rush the Lord in anything.

The Lord is always on time to give us what we need.

We live in a world where many people love to rush to do things.

Doing things too quickly can surely cause you and me to regret it.

The Lord will never rush you and me to confess and repent of our sins unto Him.

The Lord will never rush anyone to believe in Him.

The Lord is not in a rush to punish anyone who sins against Him.

The Lord is not in a rush to come back again, because He wants to save as many people as He can from being lost in sin.

You and I, who are saved in Jesus Christ, can't rush Jesus to come back again.

Jesus didn't rush you and me to choose to live for Him.

Jesus didn't rush you and me to deny ourselves and pick up our crosses to follow Him.

We can't rush the Lord to help us do anything.

We can't rush the Lord to heal us when we are sick.

We can trust the Lord to give us strength when we need it, whether we need spiritual strength, physical strength or emotional strength.

We can trust the Lord to get us out of trouble that the Lord didn't put us in.

We can trust the Lord to protect us from our enemies.

The Lord is always on time to do what he has to do for us.

Sometimes we can rush and try to get ahead of the Lord, but we can never do that.

If the Lord were to rush you and me to do what He says in His holy word, we wouldn't be ready to do it.

We would be out of whack and would not be ready and prepared to follow the Lord's instructions in His holy word.

If the Lord rushes us, we wouldn't be able to handle it.

Many people want to rush the Lord to answer their prayers.

Many people will rush the Lord to rescue them from trouble that they put themselves in.

We can't rush the Lord to fill up the church with people.

The Lord knows if we are strong enough and ready to minister to their needs without misrepresenting him.

Good Motives and Good Intentions

We need to have good motives and good intentions for Jesus' holy name sake.

We need to have good motives and good intentions in making Jesus look good, instead of making ourselves look good for doing good things.

Our motives and intentions need to always be right with the Lord.

Our motives and intentions need to always be right with one another.

Whatever we do in Jesus' name, our motives and intentions need to be good.

We need to give all the glory and praise to the Lord all the time, instead of glorifying and praising ourselves.

We are not worthy to be glorified and praised because we have sins to confess and repent of unto the Lord.

Our motives and intentions should always be about uplifting Jesus' holy name and not uplifting our names that can cause people to have some doubts.

Only the Lord is always worthy of our good motives and good intentions, because you and I can cause someone to change their minds about feeling good about us.

We need to have good motives and good intentions about wanting everyone to be saved in the Lord.

We need to have good motives and good intentions about our brothers and sisters in the Lord.

We need to have good motives and good intentions in our hearts and be right with everyone inside the church and outside the church.

If people don't have good motives and good intentions for you and me, then all that we can do is be good to them, pray for them and leave them in the Lord's hands.

Sooner or later, motives and intentions will be revealed, whether they are good motives and good intentions or bad motives and bad intentions.

We can't hide our motives and intentions from the Lord.

We can hide our true motives and true intentions from one another for a long time.

We need to pray and ask the Lord to help us to have good motives and good intentions for everyone.

The Lord hates bad motives and bad intentions, no matter who we are or whether we are in the church or not in the church.

The Lord loves our good motives and good intentions.

Doing Better in Life

Doing better in life is something that we can choose to do.

Everyone doesn't care to do better in life.

People who want to do better in life have a greater chance of doing better in life than people who don't want to do better in life.

Some people will get jealous of you and me for doing better in life.

They don't like to see you and me passing them by on our way up to prosperity.

Doing better in life is a choice that we can make, unless we are so sick that we can't do better.

As long as we are well, we can do better in life.

Many people are in good health and don't want to do better in life.

Many people are very intelligent and don't want to do better in life.

Many people are in their right minds and don't want to do better in life.

Many people don't care to try to do better in life.

We can choose to do better and be a blessing to our fellow man.

We can choose to do better and want to do the Lord's will.

We can choose to do better and love and obey the Lord.

Doing better in life is a wonderful thing to do.

Doing better in life is a good thing, especially for our loved ones to see.

Doing better in life can surely get the attention of the people who know how we used to be.

Doing better in life can add more years to your life.

Doing better in life is something great that no one can believe they will regret.

It's in the Lord's will for us to do better in life because it will prepare us for the next eternal life if we are saved in Jesus Christ.

To do better in life is to let go of the past.

To do better in life is to not make the same mistakes.

To do better in life is to not keep company with people who don't want to do better in life.

To do better in life is to not give up on our dreams.

To do better in life is to keep doing what we love to do as long as it is right to do, especially in the Lord's eyesight.

Doing better in life is the right thing to do.

Doing better in life is what a fool doesn't want to see you and I do.

That fool could be in our family and in our church.

Loving People for Who They Are

Loving people for who they are is not always easy to do when some people talk too much.

Loving people for who they are is not always easy when some people are controlling.

Loving people for who they are is not always easy to do when some people are jealous of you and me.

Loving people for who they are is not always easy to do when some people can get on our nerves.

Loving people for who they are is not always easy to do when some people believe that they are better than you and me.

Loving people for who they are is not always easy to do when some people won't love you and me for who we are.

Loving people for who they are is not always easy to do when some people don't want to change for the better.

Loving people for who they are is not always easy to do when some people just don't love you and me.

Loving people for who they are is not always easy to do when some people don't want you and me to have anything.

Loving people for who they are is not always easy to do when some people love to make you and me look bad.

Loving people for who they are is not always easy to do when some people won't like you and me if we don't let them use us.

Loving people for who they are is not always easy to do when some people love to show favoritism and not love everyone the same way.

It was not easy for Jesus Christ to love the Pharisees for who they were.

Jesus knew that the Pharisees hated him because He loved everybody.

We all want to be loved for who we are in our sinful nature.

Jesus Christ had no sins, but the Pharisees didn't love Jesus Christ for who he was — the Son of God.

Many people today don't love Jesus for who he is.

Loving people for who they are is not always easy to do when some people, even in the church, can be so phony.

Loving people for who they are is not always easy to do when some people, even in the church, can hurt you and me and don't care to ask us to forgive them.

Do We Always Listen?

Do we always listen to what someone is saying?

We can be so quick to say what we want to say and not really listen to what was said to us.

What you say means something, and what I say means something.

Do we always listen to one another before we think of what we want to say, whether it be right or wrong?

Many people are so quick to say what's on their minds, and don't care about listening to what someone else says to them.

If we truly listen to one another, we can learn something from one another.

The best way that we can learn things is to listen to what someone tells us.

Just by listening, we can learn so much about who is talking to us.

Just by listening, it can open up our eyes to see what we haven't seen before.

Just by listening, it can give us a change of heart.

Do we always listen?

Listening is always a good thing to do.

Just by listening, it can help us to mature more and more.

Just by listening, it can humble us.

Just by listening, it can cause us to feel much better.

Just by listening, it can cause us to want to do much better.

A lot of people are only concerned about what they say, and are not really listening to what someone else says.

Do we always listen to the Lord speaking to us in His holy word?

Do we always listen to the Lord speaking to us through the pastor?

Do we always listen to the Lord speaking to us through the Sabbath school teacher?

Do we always listen to the Lord speaking to us through someone singing a gospel song?

Do we always listen to the Lord speaking to us and through us to one another?

Just by listening, it can help us to make the right choices.

We need to be more quick to listen than to talk.

We learn more by listening than by talking.

Do we always listen to the Lord speaking to us through His holy spirit?

There are people who have the gift to listen, and they can tell you and me just about everything we said.

It's always good to listen to the Lord, who will never tell us anything wrong when you and I can say something wrong to someone who is listening to us.

What we say to one another can go in one ear and out the other ear and will forget what was said.

The Lord has given everyone in the church a spiritual gift to be used to build up the church to prove that we can listen to one another and draw closer to the Lord Jesus Christ.

Will Hold Against

Some people will hold against you what you've done to them in the past.

Some people won't let go of the wrongs you did to them in the past.

Some people will give you a look of unforgiveness without saying one word.

Some people will keep their distance from you and hold a grudge against you for something that happened many years ago, even though you have moved on with your life in the Lord.

You are a changed person, living your life unto the Lord every day.

Some people won't let you forget the wrongs you did to them in the past, even though you are a new creature in the Lord Jesus Christ.

Some people won't believe that you've changed for the better because they are holding your past sins against you.

What if Jesus was to hold our past sins against us from the time when we were living in our sins and just didn't know any better?

We can be so thankful that the Lord winked his eye at our ignorance.

We all have some past sins and wronged some people in our families and outside of our families.

Jesus has forgiven you and me of our past sins because we repented of our past sins, even though there are some people who just won't let go of the wrong that we did to them when we were very young and didn't do a lot of right.

The Lord will cast all of our sins into the bottom of the deepest sea.

The Lord forgives us of our past and present sins, if we repent and live for Him.

Some people just don't want to forgive you and me for doing them wrong in the past, even though you and I have moved on in our lives.

Jesus won't remind us of all of the wrongs that we did to Him in the past.

If there is someone who deserves to not forgive you and me of our past sins, it's surely Jesus Christ, who cannot do anyone wrong.

If Jesus doesn't hold any wrongs against us, then who are you and I to hold people's past sins against them when we have our own sins to repent unto the Lord.

No One is Better than Anyone Else

No one is better than anyone else.

We all need to eat good food.

We all need to drink clean water.

We all need to take a shower.

We all need to brush our teeth.

No one is better than anyone else.

We all breathe the same air.

We all need to put on some clothes.

We all need to wear our shoes.

We can all tell a lie.

We can all tell the truth.

We all have a shadow that follows us wherever we go.

No one is better than anyone else.

We all have a body.

We all have a soul.

We all have a heart.

We all have a mind.

No one is better than anyone else.

We can all grieve.

We can all laugh.

We can all sneeze.

We can all cough.

We can all get sick.

We can all be disappointed.

We all need some encouragement.

No one is better than anyone else.

We can all get a heartache.

We can all get angry.

We can all say something wrong.

We can all make some mistakes.

We can all do something wrong.

We can all do something right.

We all have motives.

We all have intentions.

We can all feel guilty.

We can all dream.

We can all hope for something.

We all have a destiny.

We can all choose right from wrong.

We can all die.

We all want to be accepted.

No one is better than anyone else.

Jesus Christ paid the cost for all of us.

Salvation is given to all of us.

We can all confess and repent of our sins to Jesus Christ.

Jesus loves all of us the same.

No one is better than anyone else.

We were all created in the image of God.

We are all human beings.

We can all feel good.

We can all feel bad.

We all were born in sin.

We can all change.

We all have a name.

We all want to be in good health.

We all have a habit.

No one is better than anyone else.

We all need love.

None of us know it all.

We all can't do everything.

God put His law in everyone's heart.

We are all ignorant about something.

We were all in our mother's womb.

We were all born naked.

No one is better than anyone else.

We all want to be free.

Jesus wants to set us all free from the devil's lies.

No one is better than anyone else.

The Gospel of Jesus Christ is for all of us.

Jesus can cleanse us all in His precious blood that was shed on the cross to save us all from our sins.

No one is better than anyone else in this world.

We will all leave this world and take nothing to the grave.

We all need the Lord.

We all have some questions.

We all have organs in our bodies.

We are all visible.

We all have something in common—God made us all.

Last Chance

Today may be someone's last chance to talk right.

Today may be someone's last chance to act right.

Today may be someone's last chance to get it right with someone else.

Today may be someone's last chance to do right.

Today may be someone's last chance to live right.

Today may be someone's last chance to think right.

Today may be someone's last chance to go the extra mile.

Today may be someone's last chance to make up for some Lost Time.

Today may be someone's last chance to tell the truth.

Today may be someone's last chance to know the truth.

Today may be someone's last chance to go back home.

Today may be someone's last chance to make amends.

Today may be someone's last chance to do what you say.

Today may be someone's last chance to win a game.

Today may be someone's last chance to say that you are wrong.

Today may be someone's last chance to turn around and go back the other way.

Today may be someone's last chance to walk away from danger.

Today may be someone's last chance to get out of trouble.

Today may be someone's last chance to believe in Jesus Christ.

Today may be someone's last chance to confess and repent unto Jesus Christ.

Today may be someone's last chance to be saved in Jesus Christ.

Today may be someone's last chance to give all the glory and praise to Jesus Christ.

Today may be someone's last chance to deny oneself, pick up their cross and follow Jesus Christ.

Today may be someone's last chance to humble oneself unto Jesus Christ.

Today may be someone's last chance to live.

Today may be someone's last chance to read the Bible.

Today may be someone's last chance to believe the Bible's truth.

Today may be someone's last chance to make it right with anyone they've offended.

Today may be yours and my last chance to let go of anything that can cause our souls to be lost.

That was Used the Wrong Way

Many people have gotten badly hurt by religion that was used the wrong way.

Many people still do get hurt today by religion that is used to control people.

Religion being used the wrong way will surely damage anyone who doesn't read and study the Bible for themselves.

Some people will pretend to be religious to make money.

Many people have gotten used up by so-called religious people who don't live what they preach.

Many people have gotten deceived by so-called religious people who don't live what they teach. Many people have gotten badly disappointed by religion that was used the wrong way.

The Bible says that pure religion is to visit the widows and fatherless children.

Many people will claim to be religious, but they don't visit the widows and fatherless children.

If there are any widows and fatherless children in your church, then you should visit them if you can and help them if you can.

Many people have gotten brainwashed by so-called religious people who don't live what they say about the Lord Jesus Christ.

Many so-called religious people will use religion to try to play God.

Many so-called religious people will use religion to try to get rich.

Many so-called religious people will use religion to try to make a good name for themselves.

Many people use religion in the wrong way to get popularity in the church.

Many people have been distressed by so-called religious people who love to take and not give back.

Many people have gotten discouraged by religion that was used the wrong way, which caused them to get confused about whether they are truly living right unto the Lord Jesus Christ.

Many people today are using religion in the wrong way and don't even realize it in their body language that can very often show whether they are religious or not religious.

Many so-called religious people will twist and turn the Bible scriptures to their own benefit to gain prosperity.

Many people today will say that they are religious and use it in the wrong way to look so holy and righteous, when they are full of themselves and will sooner or later be revealed inside and outside the church.

Jesus Carried Our Baggage

Jesus carried our baggage of mistakes on the cross.

Jesus carried our baggage of unbelief on the cross.

Jesus carried our baggage of flaws on the cross.

Jesus carried our baggage of bad habits on the cross.

Jesus carried our baggage of hereditary Tendencies on the cross.

Jesus carried our baggage of grief on the cross.

Jesus carried our baggage of pain on the cross.

Jesus carried our baggage of disappointments on the cross.

Jesus carried our baggage of shame on the cross.

Jesus carried our baggage of guilt on the cross.

Jesus carried our baggage of pretense on the cross.

Jesus carried our baggage of lies on the cross.

Jesus carried our baggage of deception on the cross.

Jesus carried our baggage of jealousy of the cross.

Jesus carried our baggage of pride on the cross.

Jesus carried our baggage of misfortunes on the cross.

Jesus carried our baggage of lack of self-control on the cross.

Jesus carried our baggage of prejudice on the cross.

Jesus carried our baggage of grudges on the cross.

Jesus carried our baggage of fear on the cross.

Jesus carried our baggage of ignorance on the cross.

Jesus carried our baggage of selfishness on the cross.

When Jesus Christ, our Lord, rose from the grave, He emptied our baggage and put His love in it.

When Jesus rose from the grave, He emptied our baggage and put His humility in it.

When Jesus rose from the grave, He emptied our baggage and put His mercy in it.

When Jesus rose from the grave, He emptied our baggage and put His holiness in it.

When Jesus rose from the grave, He emptied our baggage and put His righteousness in it.

When Jesus rose from the grave, He emptied our baggage and put His peace in it.

When Jesus rose from the grave, He emptied our baggage and put His truth in it.

When Jesus rose from the grave, He emptied our baggage and put His grace in it.

When Jesus rose from the grave, He emptied our baggage and put His victory in it.

A Woman Can

A woman can look so beautiful.

A woman can have the most beautiful smile.

A woman can cause a man to be successful.

A woman can make a weak man strong.

A woman can do almost anything that a man can do.

A woman can do some things that a man can't do.

A woman can take good care of her children without a man.

A woman can be very interesting to talk to.

A woman can be good to be around.

A woman can be very brilliant.

A woman can be a genius.

A woman change a man for the better.

A woman can fight like a man.

A woman can love more deeply than a man.

A woman can cause a man to feel on top of the world.

A woman can be strong when the going gets tough.

A woman can dress up to get a lot of attention.

A woman can build a man up when he has been torn down.

A woman can encourage her children to do great things.

A woman can be a better communicator than a man.

A woman can have more feelings than a man.

A woman can sense things better than a man.

A woman is the greatest gift from God for a man to not deny.

A woman can get a man's attention on his worst day.

A woman can cause a man to go the extra mile.

A woman can cause a strong man to become weak.

A woman can cause a man to behave much better.

A woman can cause a man to dress better.

A woman can cause a man to straighten up and do right.

A woman can be a trophy to a man.

A woman can be so wonderful to love.

A woman can be so captivating to a man.

A woman can be so careful to reject a man she is not interested in.

A woman can be very clever to get what she wants from a man.

A woman can be more giving than a man.

A woman can be more forgiving than a man.

A woman can be more trustworthy than a man.

A woman can be more cheerful than a man.

A woman can love the Lord more than a man.

A woman can get up and go more than a man.

A woman can have more faith in the Lord than a man.

A woman can obey the Lord more than a man.

A woman can have more compassion than a man.

A woman can have more heart than a man.

A woman can work harder than a man.

A woman can be more educated than a man.

A woman can have better understanding than a man.

A woman can see things that a man can't see.

A woman can be more careful than a man.

A woman can be more successful than a man.

A woman can figure out things that a man can't figure out.

A woman can be more helpful than a man.

A woman can be more hopeful than a man.

When God created a woman for a man, it was no mistake.

Sin entered into this world through a man and not through a woman.

Sin entered into this world through a man who ate the forbidden fruit.

A man can't blame a woman for his own actions.

Adam and Eve's eyes were opened to sin right after Adam bit into the forbidden fruit.

We men can't live in this world without women.

We men would die out and have no existence without women giving birth to us human beings.

God said that it is not good for man to be alone.

God created a woman to give birth, and no man can do that.

This comes to show that a woman can do a miraculous, wonderful and profound thing that no man can do.

A woman can help a man to be transparent.

A woman can help a man to give his heart to the Lord.

A woman can be a man's best friend.

A woman can be everything to a man.

A woman can hurt a man's pride.

A woman can cause a man to feel like a king.

A woman can cause a man to feel very important.

A woman can cause a man to feel like nothing.

A woman can be so good to a man.

A woman can cause a man to feel powerful.

A woman can be very helpful to a man.

A woman can help a man to come back to the Lord.

A woman can look very desirable to a man.

A woman can be like a dream to a man.

A woman can cause a man to love her more than anything in this world.

A woman can be very powerful and do great things.

A woman can cause a man to do anything for her.

A woman can be who God requires her to be.

A woman can be God's wonderful friend.

A woman can be beautiful on the outside and on the inside.

You Didn't Cast Me Out

I am so glad, O Lord, that You didn't cast me out when I came to You with a tormented mind.

O Lord, you set me free from a tormented mind so I could worship You and give you all the praise and glory.

O Lord, you didn't cast me out when I came to You all broken up in shame and guilt.

O Lord, you didn't cast me out when I came to You with an unclean spirit that tortured my soul day and night.

I am so glad, O Lord, that you didn't cast me out when I came to You with a sincere heart to want to give up the things that failed me.

O Lord, you didn't cast me out when I came to you with nothing good in me — You accepted me with joy and changed my life to do Your holy will.

Oh Lord, you didn't cast me out when I came to You so messed up in sin that You set me free from living in.

O Lord, you didn't cast me out when I came to You with my ignorance that you winked your eye at.

O Lord, you didn't cast me out when I came to You with my weakness that you strengthened for me to resist the devil's temptations.

O Lord, you didn't cast me out when I came to You with a little, simple prayer — You looked down on me and answered my prayers from heaven above.

O Lord, you didn't cast me out when I came to you in my poor spirit — You made my spirit rich so that I could be a witness of You to all the world.

What Matters the Most

Looking beautiful is not everything.

Having big muscles is not everything.

Being successful is not everything.

What matters the most is one's character.

Being a hero is not everything.

Having trophies is not everything.

Having awards is not everything.

What matters the most is not boasting about oneself.

Being rich is not everything.

Being educated is not everything.

Being brilliant is not everything.

What matters the most is helping people who need help, no matter the color of their skin.

Being famous is not everything.

Being skillful is not everything.

Being great is not everything.

What matters the most is to love people.

Being a pastor is not everything.

Being a gospel singer is not everything.

Being a Sabbath school teacher is not everything.

What matters the most is living right unto Jesus Christ.

Being an elder is not everything.

Being a deacon is not everything.

Being a missionary, evangelist and a community service worker is not everything.

What matters the most is keeping Jesus Christ above oneself.

Going to church is not everything.

Returning tithes and offerings are not everything.

Giving testimonies is not everything.

Being a church leader is not everything.

Having spiritual gifts is not everything.

What matters the most is being saved in Jesus Christ.

Having a big, beautiful house is not everything.

Being in great health is not everything.

Having your own business is not everything.

Having a career is not everything.

Having material things is not everything.

What matters the most is being fair with everybody, respecting everybody, and being honest with everybody.

What matters the most is loving Jesus Christ and loving our neighbors, beginning in our own homes where our families truly know us to be good or bad.

Even our pets can sense whether we are good or bad.

Innocent Until Proven Guilty

Someone can say that you or I told a lie, without having any proof that we were lying.

You and I are innocent until proven guilty.

Someone can believe that he or she is so right when they say that you and I told a lie, but they have no proof that they are correct.

It doesn't matter who assumes you and I are guilty of what they believe to be true about us.

You and I can tell the truth about what we said to someone, when that person can tell someone else what we said.

That someone else can believe that you and I told a lie, when the person we originally told the truth to believed that we told him or her the truth.

I told the truth to someone about what I did, and that someone told someone else who believed that I lied about what I said I did.

The person I told the truth to believed me, even though she had no proof about what I told her I did.

God was my witness and saw what I did, and I felt good about telling the truth, regardless of being called a liar.

If someone who knows you calls you a liar without any proof, then there is some strong mistrust in his or her heart against you.

I felt that strong mistrust in that person when I heard him say that what I said that I did was a lie.

I was on a group conference prayer line phone call when I heard him say those cold-hearted words about me and made me look like a liar to the other people who were also listening to the call.

As I listened to him say that what I said was not true, I did not respond to what he said.

He didn't know that I was on the conference call, or maybe he just didn't care if I heard what he said about me at that time.

I know that I am innocent before the Lord, who knows that I told the truth like I know that I told the truth.

I am innocent until proven guilty, and he couldn't prove that I was guilty of lying to my sister in Jesus Christ.

To Guard

We need to pray and ask the Lord to guard our minds so that we don't think about things that are not good to think about.

We need to pray and ask the Lord to guard our eyes so that we do not look at what is not good to look at.

We need to pray and ask the Lord to guard our ears so that we do not listen to what is not good to listen to.

We need to pray and ask the Lord to guard our tongues, so that we do not say what is not good to say.

We need to pray and ask the Lord to guard our hands, so that we do not hold onto what is not good to hold onto.

We need to pray and ask the Lord to guard our feet, so that we do not walk where it's not good to walk.

We need to pray and ask the Lord to guard our hearts, so that we do not feel what is not good to feel.

We need to pray and ask the Lord to guard our lives, so that we do not live them doing our own will.

We need to pray and ask the Lord to guard our souls, so that we are not lost in sin.

No one can guard you and me better than the Lord, who gives us a guardian angel.

The Lord is our best Guardian to guard us from eternal death for being saved in Him.

We need to pray and ask the Lord to guard our free will choices so that we do not choose to be selfish.

We need to pray and ask the Lord to guard our existence, so that we can be like him in this temporary world.

Jesus guards all of his angels, who chose not to rebel against Him up in heaven.

Jesus guards the heavens against the fallen angels so that they can never enter into the heavens where you and I will enter one day for being saved in Jesus.

The holy angels forever know that the Lord is the guardian over the seen and unseen.

The holy angels forever know that the Lord is the guardian over all existence, except hell, where the devil and his angels and all the wicked will go to with no protection from their eternal fate.

Living This Life

Living this life is nothing good, like the eternal life.

Living this life is nothing wonderful, like the eternal life.

Living this life is nothing glorious, like the eternal life.

Living this life is nothing great, like the eternal life.

We don't truly know what living is until we receive eternal life.

Living the eternal life will be beyond our greatest dreams.

Living the eternal life will be beyond our greatest ambitions.

Living the eternal life will be beyond our greatest achievements.

Living the eternal life will be beyond our greatest accomplishments.

Living the eternal life will be beyond our greatest wants.

Living the eternal life will be beyond our greatest needs.

We must be saved in Jesus Christ to live the eternal life.

The eternal life is Jesus Christ.

Living the eternal life will be beyond our greatest desires.

Many people believe that they are living the good life in this world where life is short-lived.

Many people believe that life is so great in this world where tomorrow is not promised for us to live.

Many people believe that this life is what's going on.

The eternal life is forever more greater than this life on Earth.

The eternal life is forever more glorious than this life on Earth.

The eternal life is forever more wonderful than this life on Earth.

Jesus gave up His life on the cross and rose from the grave to give us eternal life if we are saved in Him.

Jesus Christ is coming back again to give eternal life to all who are saved in Him.

Living this life is nothing prosperous, like the eternal life.

Living this life is nothing peaceful, like the eternal life.

Living this life is nothing loving, like the eternal life.

Living this life is nothing victorious, like the eternal life.

Living this life is nothing beautiful, like the eternal life.

Living this life is nothing spectacular, like the eternal life.

Living this life is nothing magnificent, like the eternal life.

Living this life is nothing refreshing, like the eternal life.

Living this life is nothing wealthy, like the eternal life.

Living this life is nothing joyful, like the eternal life.

Living this life is nothing lawful, like the eternal life.

Living this life is nothing free, like the eternal life.

The eternal life is forevermore better than living in this life.

People believe that living this life is heaven.

Many people believe that living this life is all that they have to live.

The eternal was here before this life ever existed.

The eternal life was made flesh and lived among short-lived people.

Living this life is nothing worthy, like the eternal life.

Living this life is nothing healthy, like the eternal life.

Living this life is nothing truthful, like the eternal life.

Living this life is nothing right, like the eternal life.

Living this life is nothing cheerful, like the eternal life.

Living this life is nothing rewarding, like the eternal life.

Living this life is nothing fulfilling, like the eternal life.

Living this life is nothing mystical, like the eternal life.

Living this life is nothing united, like the eternal life.

Living this life is nothing transparent, like the eternal life.

Living this life is nothing poetic, like the eternal life.

Living this life is nothing expressive, like the eternal life.

Living this life is nothing artistic, like the eternal life.

The eternal life is forevermore spiritual than living in this life.

The eternal life is forevermore righteous than living in this life.

The eternal life is forevermore holy than living in this life.

The eternal life is forevermore hopeful than living in this life.

The eternal life is forevermore graceful than living in this life.

Living this life is nothing meaningful, like the eternal life.

Living this life is nothing simple, like the eternal life.

Living this life is nothing lived, like the eternal life.

Living this life is nothing justified, like the eternal life.

Living this life is nothing respectful, like the eternal life.

Living this life is nothing kind, like the eternal life.

Living this life is nothing gentle, like the eternal life.

Living this life is nothing balanced, like the eternal life.

Living this life is nothing faithful, like the eternal life.

Living this life is nothing temperance, like the eternal life.

Living this life is nothing pure, like the eternal life.

Living this life is nothing supernatural, like the eternal life.

Jesus Christ, our Lord and Savior, is eternal life forevermore beyond living in this life that is like a bubble that will burst when it touches down on the ground.

A lot of people don't believe that there is an eternal life.

They believe that this life on Earth is the only life to live.

The Bible lets us know that there is an eternal life to live in Jesus Christ.

If we believe in Jesus Christ, we shall be saved to receive eternal life when Jesus comes back again with all of His angels.

The Living and the Dead

The living can breathe, eat and drink.

The dead can't breathe, eat and drink.

The living can hear, see, taste, touch and smell.

The dead can't hear, see, taste, touch and smell.

The living can talk and walk and run and can go here and there.

The dead can't talk and walk and run and can't go here and there.

The living are conscious and know what is going on.

The dead are not conscious and do not know what is going on.

The living can reason things through and can make choices.

The dead can't reason and can't make choices.

The living can laugh and cry and grieve.

The dead can't laugh and cry and grieve.

The living can dream and prosper.

The dead can't dream and can't Prosper.

The living can smile and sing.

The dead can't smile and can't sing.

The living can work.

The dead can't work.

The living have a chance to live right unto the Lord.

The dead have run out of chances.

The living can pray to the Lord.

The dead can't pray to the Lord.

The living can worship the Lord.

The dead can't Worship the Lord.

The living can learn.

The dead can't learn anything.

The living can love.

The dead can't love.

The living can think.

The dead can't think about anything.

The living can harm you and me.

The dead can't harm you and me.

The living can lie to you and me.

The dead can't lie to you and me.

The living can kill you and me.

The dead can't kill you and me.

The living can talk to you and me.

 The dead can't talk to you and me.

The living can see you and me.

The dead can't see you and me.

The living can hear you and me.

The dead can't hear you and me.

The living can smell you and me.

The day I can't smell you and me.

The living can touch you and me.

The dead can't touch you and me.

The living can confess and repent unto the Lord.

The dead can't confess and repent and to the Lord.

The living can do a lot of things.

The dead can't do anything.

The living know a lot of things.

The dead know nothing.

The living can say a lot of words.

The dead can't say anything.

If the dead were alive, there would be no dead bodies in the graves.

Death wouldn't exist at all if dead people could still be alive for you and me to see them, talk to them, live with them and do things with them.

If the dead were still alive, then the dead would have no need to appear and then disappear before us.

The dead would have no limits and could live with us if they were still alive.

The dead are limited to the grave of permanent unconsciousness until Jesus Christ raises the righteous dead to receive eternal life and raises the wicked dead to receive eternal death.

Only the living have life.

The dead have no life.

Life can be great and life can be burdensome for the living.

The dead have no life to be great or burdensome.

The living are truly alive.

The dead are dead and have a permanent fate that the living can't change with theories of being able to talk to the dead, who the fallen angels will appear to look like and talk like.

If our dead loved ones had the power to come back to life, then why would they appear to us and then disappear before us when they really want to live with us again and not be apart from us?

The living love to be with their loved ones and not apart from their loved ones.

Even a wicked man can love to be with someone who is alive.

If our dead loved ones had the power to live again, then why would they want to look down on us from heaven when they could live with us so we would not have to grieve over them?

Only the living have life that the dead can't live, and we need to be conscious and aware of the truth and not a lie.

The Wings of Life

The wings of Life can fly us across the skies of Longevity, if we don't break the wings of obedience unto the Lord.

The wings of life can fly us across the skies of success to last all of our Lives, if we don't break the wings of giving all the glory and praise unto the Lord.

The wings of life can fly us across the skies of peace of mind, if we don't break the wings of keeping our minds on the Lord in this troubled world.

The wings of life can fly us to great spiritual heights across the skies of maturing in the Lord, if we don't break the wings of reading and studying God's holy word to help us to mature in the Lord.

The wings of life can fly us across the skies of ministering to one another about the Lord, if we don't break the wings of keeping the Lord first above our ministering that the Lord gave us to do to build up his church.

The wings of life can fly us across the skies of humility unto the Lord, if we don't break the wings of denying ourselves and picking up our crosses to follow Jesus Christ, who humbled Himself even unto death on the cross to save you and me from our sins.

The wings of life can fly us across the skies of joy in the Lord, if we don't break the wings of keeping our trust in the Lord to give us an unspeakable joy, even in our trials.

The wings of life can fly us across the skies of love for one another, if we don't break the wings of forgiving one another for the Lord to forgive us.

The wings of life can fly us across the skies of freedom from distress, if we don't break the wings of giving all of our burdens to the Lord to make us feel as light as a feather floating in the sky.

The wings of life can fly us across the skies of a renewed life in the Lord, if we don't break the wings of repenting of our sins unto the Lord for us to turn away from living in sin.

The wings of life have flown many people across the skies of wealth because Jesus is the pilot who never gets tired on His flights.

The wings of life have flown many people across the skies of not giving up on their dreams because Jesus is the pilot who never gets sleepy on His flights.

The wings of life have flown many people across the skies of hope because Jesus is the pilot who never gets sick on his flights.

The wings of life have flown many people across the skies of success because Jesus is the pilot who never gets irritated on His flights.

The wings of life have flown many people across the skies of a better life to live because Jesus is the pilot who never gets intoxicated on His flights.

The wings of life can fly you and me across the skies of being saved in Jesus Christ, if we don't break the wings of believing in Jesus Christ.

The Best

The best songs to sing are songs about the Lord Jesus Christ, who the holy angels sing about forever and ever.

The best books to write are books about the Lord, and the holy Bible book is proof of that.

The best one to talk to is the Lord Jesus Christ, who understands all things and has the answer to all things.

The best work that we can do is work for the Lord Jesus Christ, who is the best boss that anyone can ever have.

Jesus will never stress us out, He will never lay us off and the Lord will never fire you and me who can quit on Him.

The best poems to recite are poems about the Lord.

The best poems to write are poems about the Lord Jesus Christ.

The best place to go is to church to worship the Lord Jesus Christ with our spiritual brothers and sisters, assembling ourselves together before the Lord and giving Him all the glory and praise for what He does for us every day.

The best TV programs to watch are programs about the Lord, who is the good news to all the world.

The best thing to do is to do the Lord's holy will that has no flaws of sin.

The best life to live is a life unto Jesus Christ.

We will have no regrets for living our lives unto the Lord.

The best one to follow every day is the Lord Jesus Christ.

Jesus will never lead us to be lost in our sins.

He will always lead you and me to be safe in Him to go back to heaven with Him when He comes back again.

The best food we can eat is the spiritual food of Jesus Christ.

His holy word is the best food to satisfy our hungry souls.

The best water to drink is the living waters that are spiritually pure and will quench our thirsty souls so that we are never spiritually thirsty in this dehydrated world of living in perilous times.

The best one we can listen to is the Lord Jesus Christ, who speaks all truth to us with love through His holy spirit.

The best clothes we can wear are the clothes of Jesus Christ's righteousness that will never wear out or get dirty on us, when our clothes are like filthy rags and show the filth of our wrongdoing.

The best race that we can run is the Christian race that will cross us over the finish line of getting our prize of eternal life in Jesus Christ.

We Were Born in this World and Will One Day Die

We were born in this world and will one day die, to be like a good movie that ends.

We were born in this world and will one day die, to be like the grass that dries up.

We were born in this world and will one day die, to be like a shadow that fades away across the landscape.

We were born in this world and will one day die, to be like the leaves that fall off the trees.

We were born in this world and will one day die, to be like a light bulb that blows out.

We were born in this world and will one day die, to be like water that runs down the drain.

We were born in this world and will one day die, to be like the snow that melts away.

We were born in this world and will one day die, to be like shoes that wear out.

We were born in this world and will one day die, to be like paper that burns to ashes.

We were born in this world and will one day die to be like a lost memory.

We were born in this world and will one day die, to be like a glass that's dropped onto a concrete floor and breaks into pieces.

We were born in this world and will one day die, to be like losing a treasure and never finding it again.

We were born in this world and will one day die to live again when Jesus Christ comes back to give us eternal life if we are saved in Him.

We were born in this world and will one day die, to be like a bubble that bursts.

We were born in this world and will one day die, to be like a car that breaks down on the highway.

We were born in this world and will one day die, to be like going into a dark cave and not being able to find a way out.

We were born in this world and will one day die, to be like a candle light going out.

We were born in this world and will one day die, to be like getting lost in the desert on a very cold night.

We were born in this world and will one day die, to be like waste being flushed down the toilet.

We were born in this world and will one day die, unless Jesus Christ comes back before we die, for us to be change from mortal to immortal if we are saved in Him.

We were born in this world and will one day die, to be like a falling star disappearing in the night.

We were born in this world and will one day die, hopefully being saved in Jesus Christ who got the victory over death and the grave when He rose from the grave for you and me to live forever and ever with Him.

Jesus Foreknew All Things

Jesus foreknew that His heavenly father would send Him to be the savior of the world.

Jesus foreknew this world's past, present and future.

When Jesus lived here on Earth, he spoke the people's language so the people could understand Him.

Jesus spoke the words of their present-day language so the people could relate to Him.

Even before Jesus came to this world, he foreknew that He couldn't speak the words of today's world technology to the people.

They would not have understood what a cell phone is.

They would not have understood what a computer is.

They would not have understood what an airplane is.

They would not have understood what a train is.

They would not have understood what a car is.

They would not have understood what a truck is.

They would not have understood what a TV is.

Jesus foreknew all of these things up in heaven, where Jesus was predestined to come to this sinful world to save us from our sins.

We people today are like the people back in the Bible days when it comes to us not knowing the language and technology of other worlds that Jesus foreknew before He created those other worlds.

We are so very far behind those other worlds with the technology that we have that can't reach those other worlds.

Jesus foreknew that our sins would limit us from those other worlds until He comes back again to take us to heaven so that we can also visit those other worlds if we are saved in Him.

Jesus Christ, Our Lord and Savior, foreknew all things in heaven and throughout the universe because He is before all things that He created.

If Jesus had spoken to the people back in the Bible days about this world's science and technology today, they would probably have believed that Jesus had lost His mind.

Jesus foreknew that He couldn't tell them what they wouldn't understand.

Today, Jesus can't tell us about what is going on in other worlds because He foreknew we wouldn't understand because of our sinful nature.

Jesus can't tell us about what is going on up in heaven because of our sinful nature.

We can believe that we know what is going on in heaven when we are not there yet.

Jesus foreknew all things, when we can only speculate about things that we don't know until the Lord gives us evidence.

We Black Human Beings

We black human beings were created in the image of God, who also loves us black human beings.

Many of us black human beings love our light skin, light brown skin, medium brown skin, dark brown skin and dark skin complexions.

We black human beings are profound souls with a strong will to live and survive against injustice and prejudice.

Our black ancestors are the crowns on the heads of our black history that sings joyful and victorious songs about us still existing today.

God smiled down from heaven and said, "I will create black human beings to populate the Earth with black men, women, boys and girls."

We black human beings are like the ocean waves splashing against the hard rocks of injustice, prejudice and discrimination that we black human beings face every day.

We black human beings are like beautiful furniture in the house of this world, where the dust of hatred against us covers over us every day.

We black human beings are like the seasons that change — we go through the changes of not knowing when the policemen will come our way to shoot us down when many of us are innocent.

We black human beings are like the full white moonlight's glow — we glow our gifts, talents and skills all through the dark nights of oppression.

We black human beings are like a beautiful pathway that other races of people can walk down and see how our black ancestors prosper in this great nation.

We black human beings are like the beautiful rainbow in the sky so that people of other races can see that we black human beings have different complexions and like a rainbow of people up in the sky of life.

We black human beings are the soul music to melt people's hearts to change for the better to bring love, peace, unity and equality.

We black human beings are beautiful to God, who wonderfully made us.

As long as we are beautiful to God, it doesn't matter what people of other races think of us day after day.

The sunlight treats us black human beings right every day.

The moonlight treats us black human beings right every night.

The great blue sky treats us black human beings right every day and every night.

Nature treats us black human beings right all of the time.

We black human beings are like a deep mystery to many people of other races, and many of them can't solve our black presence in this world because many of them were taught that we black human beings evolved from apes.

Our black ancestors are like a bridge that every black man, woman, boy and girl can cross over to get to the opportunity of an education.

We black human beings are like a good movie, and can move people to cry, laugh, dream, love and not give up on hope for a brighter day.

God created us black human beings for His pleasure.

We black human beings had to go through trials and tribulations that our black ancestors went through to make life better for us black human beings today.

God is pleased with us black human beings all around the world, for we are countless like the stars in the universe for God to marvel at us every day.

We black human beings are destined to live in this world with countless other races of people who God commands us black human beings to love every day, regardless of them looking so different from us.

We black human beings are like the very huge iceberg that sunk the Titanic ship.

Our ancestors broke through the Titanic ships of slavery for us black human beings to be in our rescue boats of democracy today.

God is for us and not against us black human beings to break through the past to heal in the present and to spearhead many good things for us black human beings in the future to come.

We black human beings are like a hot iron to iron out the wrinkles of stereotyping that made many innocent black human beings victims of violence and death, especially in this nation.

We black human beings' humbled and determined ancestors climbed high mountains so us black people can be where we are all at today in this prosperous land.

We were carried on the backs of our black ancestors who plowed with a mule in the hot sun to plant crops, picked cotton under the hot sun in the fields and worked hard in factories.

Our black ancestors' hard work was technology in their day to help make this nation great today.

We black human beings are so blessed to live in this world with Christian people of every race that have helped us black human beings to know that we are not alone and can hold up the flag of peace over our heads.

Many white Christian people joined in our march for justice and equality.

We black human beings can truly thank God for good people of every race.

Those good people cheered for us black human beings to make it this far in life, and they help us celebrate our victories over the past heartlessness and misfortune.

We black human beings who are saved in Jesus Christ will be made like the angels when we go to heaven when Jesus comes back again.

It's the Holy Spirit

It's the Holy Spirit who convicts us of our sins.

It's the Holy Spirit who converts us to live right unto the Lord.

It's the Holy Spirit who helps us to make good choices.

It's the Holy Spirit who encourages us to deny ourselves and pick up our crosses and follow Jesus Christ.

It's the Holy Spirit who teaches us all truths.

It's the Holy Spirit who takes our prayers up to heaven before God.

It's the Holy Spirit who inspired men to write the Bible.

It's the Holy Spirit who connects us to the Lord.

It's the Holy Spirit who got the Virgin Mary pregnant to birth Jesus Christ, the Son of God.

It's the Holy Spirit who helped Jesus to remember the scriptures to speak to the devil when Jesus was in the wilderness for forty days and nights.

It's the Holy Spirit who raised Jesus from the grave.

It's the Holy Spirit who gives us spiritual gifts.

It's the Holy Spirit who changes our hearts to do the Lord's will.

It's the Holy Spirit who comforts our souls.

It's the Holy Spirit who helps us to love and obey the Lord.

It's the Holy Spirit who gives us a clear conscience to know that the Lord will save us from our sins if we confess and repent.

It's the Holy Spirit who goes the extra mile to bring us to the Lord when we don't deserve it.

It's the Holy Spirit who helps us to see the truth about ourselves.

It's the Holy Spirit who helps us to see the truth about others.

It's the Holy Spirit who helps us to surrender our hearts to the Lord.

It's the Holy Spirit who warns us to think before we talk so we don't say the wrong words.

It's the Holy Spirit who warns us to think before we do anything so that we don't do something wrong.

It's the Holy Spirit who we should always listen to every day that the Holy Spirit speaks to us through God's holy word.

It's the Holy Spirit who we should always listen to every day that the Holy Spirit speaks to us through good people.

It's the Holy Spirit who we should always listen to every day that the Holy Spirit speaks to us through nature.

It's the Holy Spirit who was in on the creation of heaven and earth.

It's the Holy Spirit who was in on the creation of Adam and Eve.

It's the Holy Spirit who was in on the creation of all things that exist.

It's the Holy Spirit who is in the Trinity of the Godhead.

It's the Holy Spirit who gives God's goodness to all the world.

It's the Holy Spirit who is keeping the devil from destroying this whole world.

It's the Holy Spirit who will put the Lord's seal on you and me and on all who are saved in the Lord to go to heaven when our Lord and Savior Jesus Christ comes back again.

It's the Holy Spirit who takes our minds up in the spiritual heights of God and then brings our minds back down to earth for us to humble ourselves.

The Righteous
Will Barely Be Saved

If the righteous will barely be saved, then there is no way possible for a wicked person to be saved and go to heaven.

The fallen angels were not spared to live in heaven after they rebelled against God.

The Bible says that if we believe in Jesus Christ, we shall be saved.

It doesn't mean that once we are saved we are always saved.

We can only be saved in Jesus one day at a time.

Many people were once saved in Jesus and then they turned their backs on Him and strayed away.

How can anyone be saved in Jesus Christ and live in sin?

How can anyone be saved in Jesus while living in adultery?

How can anyone be saved in Jesus while telling lies?

How can anyone be saved in Jesus while fornicating?

How can anyone be saved in Jesus while stealing?

How can anyone be saved in Jesus while killing?

How can anyone be saved in Jesus while disobeying their parents?

We can't be saved in Jesus if we are gossiping.

We can't be saved in Jesus if we are greedy for worldly gain.

We can't be saved in Jesus if we believe that we are self-made.

We can't be saved in Jesus if we are proud and arrogant.

The righteous will barely be saved like the Bible says.

Jesus will save us, if we confess and repent and turn away from living in our sins.

God's goodness leads us to repent, but everybody will not repent and be saved in Jesus Christ.

It's easy to be saved in Jesus Christ, if we believe in Jesus Christ.

Believing in Jesus Christ is to love Him and keep His Commandments.

If the righteous will barely be saved in Jesus Christ, then there's no way possible for people who are not living right to be saved and go to heaven one day.

Righteous people are people who live right unto the Lord every day.

Don't be deceived — no unrighteous person will go to heaven.

We can't be saved in Jesus if we are living an unrighteous life.

If the righteous will barely be saved, then you and I should surely want to be saved because we love Jesus and not because we are afraid of being lost.

The righteous will barely be saved, even though many Christians live their lives like it's easy to be a Christian all the time.

There are people in the Bible who disobeyed the Lord on their Christian journey, even though they were very sincere about the Lord, they had fallen short of His glory.

This comes to show and tell us that the righteous will barely be saved.

There is no way possible for an unrepentant soul to be saved and go to heaven if the righteous will barely be saved and go to heaven.

The fallen angels refused to repent of their sins, and they fell from heaven.

Jesus loves us all and He gave up His life on the cross and rose from the grave to save us all.

It's easy for Jesus to save us if we believe in Him, even though the righteous will barely be saved and go to heaven.

This comes to show that only a few will enter into heaven when Jesus Christ comes back again.

Even though those going to heaven will be a number that no man can count, it will only be a few compared to all the people who ever lived in this world from the beginning of this world to the end of this word.

The righteous will barely be saved, and hopefully you and I will be in the few who will be made like the countless angels who number so much more than all who ever lived on this Earth and all who are living in these last days on Earth.

In Every Church

There are some true Christians in every church, even though every church doesn't preach and teach all the truth in the Bible.

There are some true Christians in every church where they love Jesus.

There are some true Christians in every church where they obey Jesus.

There are some true Christians in every church where they love all of their brothers and sisters in the Lord Jesus Christ.

There are some true Christians in every church and they put all of their trust in Jesus Christ to work things out for them.

There are some true Christians in every church where they use their spiritual gifts to build up the church.

There are some true Christians in every church where they live a holy life inside and outside the church.

There are some true Christians in every church where they live a righteous life inside and outside the church.

There are some true Christians in every church where they give all the praise and glory to the Lord Jesus Christ.

There are some true Christians in every church where they live right by example to all the world.

There are some true Christians in every church where they worship the Lord in spirit and truth.

There are some true Christians in every church even though they don't keep the holy Sabbath day of rest on the seventh day of the week.

There are some true Christians in every church where they live right like the right they know about the Lord Jesus Christ.

There are some true Christians in every church that God will judge.

There are some true Christians in every church where they please the Lord and not the world.

There are some true Christians in every church where they will go through trials for Jesus' holy name sake.

There are some true Christians in every church where they sincerely pray unto the Lord with a selfless heart.

There are some true Christians in every church where they are humble before the Lord.

There are some true Christians in every church where they are saved in Jesus Christ.

There are some true Christians in every church where they will go back to heaven with Jesus Christ when He comes back again.

There are some true Christians in every church where they are filled with the Holy Spirit.

There are some true Christians in every church, even though every church doesn't have a large congregation.

There are some true Christians in every church where they give testimonies about Jesus Christ.

Hourglass synopsis

It's God's holy spirit who gives me the words to write poetry about Jesus Christ my Lord and Savior. I wouldn't know what to write without the Holy Spirit. The Holy Spirit inspires me to write poetry according to my measure of faith and level of knowledge about my Lord Jesus Christ.

My mind is so blank without the Holy Spirit, who inspires me with the words to create my inspirational poetry. I don't take credit for what has come from the Holy Spirit, who takes my mind into the realm of spiritual things about my Lord. It's the Holy Spirit who connects me to the spiritual world beyond the real world. The Holy Spirit gives me down to earth poetry to reach up to the spiritual world of God to be like praying to God.

You can read my prose and rhyming poetry to see if it makes good sense to you. If it does make good sense to you, then you should know that it's the Holy Spirit who has given me the understanding of poetry to write about my Lord. I have no idea what the Holy Spirit will move me to write about the Lord to share with you, but hopefully you will be blessed by it.